AF243994

Mteto Nyati

BETTING
on a
DARKIE

Lifting the corporate game

KWELA BOOKS

Kwela Books,
an imprint of NB Publishers, a division of Media24 Boeke (Pty) Ltd
40 Heerengracht, Cape Town, South Africa
PO Box 879, Cape Town 8000, South Africa
www.kwela.com

Cover image: Siphiwe Mhlambi. Vector supplied by Bubushonok/Shuttershock

Cover design: Nudge Studio
Editor: Gillian Warren-Brown
Proofreader: Sean Fraser
Typography: Nazli Jacobs
Set in Wilke

Originally printed in South Africa
ISBN: 978-0-7957-0929-6 (First edition, first impression 2019)

LSiPOD: 978-0-7957-1046-9 (Second edition, first impression 2021)
Epub: 978-0-7957-0930-2
Mobi: 978-0-7957-0931-9

To those born in difficult circumstances,
dealt a bad hand, or perceived as outsiders: in the end
what makes you are your choices.

Contents

Acronyms

ANC – African National Congress

AP – Asia Pacific

AZASO – Azanian Students' Organisation

BEE – Black Economic Empowerment

BLSA – Business Leadership South Africa

BMF – Black Management Forum

BOLD – Building Organisational Leadership Depth

CBD – Central Business District

CEMA – Central Europe, Middle East and Africa

CEO – Chief Executive Officer

CFO – Chief Financial Officer

CIO – Chief Information Officer

COO – Chief Operations Officer

COSATU – Congress of South African Trade Unions

CSIR – Council for Scientific and Industrial Research

CWU – Communication Workers' Union

CXO – C-level executives, such as CEO, CFO etc.

DG – Director-General

DTI – Department of Trade and Industry

EFF – Economic Freedom Fighters

EMEA – Europe, Middle East and Africa

EXCO – Executive Committee

GM – General Manager

HQ – Headquarters

HR – Human Resources

ICT – Information and Communication Technology

IITPSA – Institute of Information Technology Professionals of South
    Africa

ISO – International Science Olympiad

IT – Information Technology

JSE – Johannesburg Stock Exchange

LTE – Long Term Evolution

MBA – Master of Business Administration

MD – Managing Director

MK – Umkhonto we Sizwe

NDP – National Development Plan

NERSA – National Energy Regulator of South Africa

OEM – Original Equipment Manufacturer

PRISM – Priority Setting Meeting

SALGA – South African Local Government Association

SITA – State Information Technology Agency

SMB – Small and Medium Business

STB – Set Top Box

TPS – Total Production Systems

USAASA – Universal Service and Access Agency of South Africa

Company Names

Afrox – African Oxygen Limited

Altron – Allied Electronics Limited

Altech UEC – division of Altron

BCX – Business Connexion

Brait – investment holding company

Cell-C – SA mobile company

Cisco – Technology company

CRF – A company that accredits best employers

Dimension Data – IT company

Divpac – Diversified Packaging, division of Nampak

Eskom – Electricity Supply Commission

FNB – First National Bank

IBM – International Business Machines

Investec – specialist banking and asset management group

Microsoft – multinational technology company

MTN – Mobile Telephone Network

Nampak – packaging company

Nedbank – financial services group

Rain – mobile data-only network

SAB – South African Breweries

SAP – multinational software corporation

SAPPI – South African Pulp and Paper Industry

Standard Bank – financial services group

Tiger Brands – packaged goods company

Tastic Rice Corporation – division of Tiger Brands

TCM – Technology Corporate Management

Telkom – South African telecommunications provider

VCP – Value Capital Partners

Vodacom – mobile communications group

WBS – Wireless Business Solutions

Foreword

I am very pleased that Mteto Nyati decided to write this book and that Kwela Books agreed to publish it.

Towards the end of the book, the author refers to an opinion piece he wrote for the South African *Sunday Times* newspaper in November 2018, in which he said:

> I had felt constrained during the Zuma years and, like many, had found it difficult to express an unequivocal position. Now I felt free to convey the importance of leaving positive footprints – of managing assets for future generations and preserving a legacy of values and ethics. And I wasn't referring to business only. Government needed proper vision.

What Nyati meant by his emphasis on vision, values and ethics was elucidated by his insertion of a particular citation: the Preamble to our National Constitution, which begins, as we know – 'We, the people of South Africa . . .', and thus binds all of us to an agreed vision and a set of agreed values, ethics and objectives.

A re-reading of that Preamble tells us much about what has gone wrong during the last 25 years of our democracy. It is also a timely reminder of how much better our country will be when, together, we act in earnest and in a sustained manner to realise the objectives set out in that Preamble.

Nyati reminds us of the challenge we face: 'The political space is a cacophony these days . . . Missing are voices of reason calling on South Africans to embrace their Constitution. We need leaders who can put forward a case for diversity and inclusion. It is not an easy message.'

According to the Oxford English Dictionary, 'cacophony' means 'a harsh discordant mixture of sounds'. Indeed, emerging out of that cacophony are charges such as that 'the negotiated 1994 settlement, obviously including the Constitution, was a betrayal of black people by Nelson Mandela and others'.

It speaks to his courage, honesty and depth of understanding that, despite this, and even in 2019, Nyati is still calling for the reconstruction and development of South Africa on the basis of 'diversity and inclusion'.

Almost twenty years ago, in 2000, speaking in Port Elizabeth at that year's National General Council (NGC) of the ANC as President of the organisation, I commented on the theme of the Council, which was about developing the kind of cadre our organisation and country needed.

Among other things, I said:

> [As the ANC] we have attracted into and continue to retain opportunists and careerists within our ranks . . . [These] join . . . with the sole aim of furthering their personal careers and using the access to state power we have as a ruling party, to enrich themselves . . . We cannot afford to have a membership driven by a value system, a morality, centred on the promotion of the

interests of these members at the expense of the fundamental and urgent interests of the millions who have twice, in 1994 and 1999, expressed the fullest confidence in the ANC...

I went on to say:

> I am talking about the need for us to develop new cadres to meet the demands imposed on us by the victories we have scored as we have pursued the objectives of the democratic revolution. I am talking here of the need for us to implement a programme focused, among other things, on the development of cadres who are truly politically committed to the all-round success of the new democratic South Africa, and properly prepared with regard to the skills our country needs to achieve that success . . . [We] have to discuss the critically important question of our interaction with and impact on the student youth, the intelligentsia and the professionals in our country. We need to ensure that these strata in our society, that either have or will have the specialised skills our country needs, at the same time have the levels of national consciousness and patriotism that will enable our people to count on them as an asset for the development and modernisation of our country, for the benefit of the masses of our people.

The reason I am pleased *Betting on a Darkie* has been written and is being published is that it covers the very same matter I addressed in 2000 in the narrow context of a meeting of a political organisation, the ANC.

In the book, Nyati discusses the possibility of developing the kind of educated, qualified cadre South Africa needs to ensure its reconstruction and development – individuals who honour our diversity while building an inclusive society; citizens who are committed to pursuing the objectives stated in the Preamble to our Constitution.

It is a matter of common cause among all our people that the radical growth and development of an inclusive South African economy is one of the urgent and strategic challenges our country faces.

Nyati argues that this objective can and must be achieved.

The eminent Irish poet, W.B. Yeats, wrote: words are lightly spoken. However, what gives weight to Nyati's words is that they are spoken by a fellow citizen who has repeatedly and practically proved his capacity as an effective economic and business change agent over a number of decades, having successfully served as an economic and business leader in a number of major domestic and international businesses.

At this point, perhaps I should say something about the contents of *Betting on a Darkie*. The book tells a very interesting story about how Nyati grew up in the Transkei in the Eastern Cape during the apartheid years, qualified as an engineer in the then Natal Province, worked at various levels in a number of companies as a developing business manager, and ended up in the position of Chief Executive Officer (CEO), to date, in major companies.

Of particular importance is that the young Nyati had to work in circumstances where, effectively, he had to serve as a pathfinder because the companies in which he worked had never had an African/black professional in their ranks above the position of ordinary labourer.

Naturally, he therefore had to overcome entrenched racial prejudice as he climbed up the managerial ranks, even as he finally reached the position of CEO in a number of companies.

Defined by the colonial and apartheid systems as the excluded and sub-human, naturally he involved himself in the liberation struggle, operating as an ANC activist. I believe all of us, as South Africans, must make an effort to understand what this book says about the impact young people had as liberation fighters and ANC activists during the post-1976 Soweto Student Uprising years.

Fortunately and quite correctly, Nyati also reflects on the important matter of his family life, which includes his parents and siblings, as well as his own wife and children.

The book is what I would call 'a semi-autobiography', which provides invaluable education about various matters, including suggestions about what our country must do to effect the fundamental economic transformation of which many speak.

Ultimately, *Betting on a Darkie* tells an inspiring story about the emergence of a role model in the context of the imperative for change agents to drive the fundamental reconstruction and development of our country so that we can deliver on the objectives detailed in the Preamble to our Constitution.

Mteto Nyati is such a model.

The story told in this book is about a humble South African who is devoted to education, and therefore the expansion of the frontiers of knowledge, who is keenly interested in using that knowledge to improve the human condition, and who understands that being educated imposes an obligation on him to stretch out a helping hand to those who are more disadvantaged than him.

This is a story about a fellow South African who is dedicated to the achievement of excellence, which drives him to hate all shoddy work. This tells all of us that this is a person whose working day will not be governed by the hours he is contracted to work, but by the quality of the product he will have produced by the end of that working day.

It is a story about a fellow national who is devoted to the values of honesty, truthfulness, objectivity and candour in the construction of good and durable human relations. This is a person devoted to principle and who therefore strives to approach his own contribution to the development of our country in a principled manner, fundamentally informed by the lessons of *ubuntu* and humaneness which he learnt at a very young age from his parents, especially his mother.

What I said in 2000 about the corruption of the ANC by the entry into its ranks of people who 'join . . . with the sole aim of furthering their personal careers and using the access to state power we have as a ruling party, to enrich themselves', was raised by Nelson Mandela at the 1997 National Conference of the ANC. It has been highlighted at all subsequent Conference Political and Organisational Reports of the ANC.

This means that for 25 years our country's governing party, the ANC, has continuously admitted and retained in its ranks exactly the kind of person who is absolutely contemptuous of the value system – selflessly to serve the people of South Africa – which has informed the ANC since its foundation 107 years ago.

Given this history, it was inevitable that a *new normal* would become established within the ANC. That *new normal* would be that the governing party actually allows its members to abuse state power to enrich themselves – against the interests of the ordinary people of our country.

The need to establish the Judicial Commissions, headed by Judges Nugent, Zondo, Mpati and Mokgoro, which have and continue to sit in our country, has arisen in reality as a direct outcome of the emergence and entrenchment in the ANC of that *new normal*.

The state capture, corruption, lawlessness, betrayal of the public trust and other ills in our society which these Commissions have exposed are a direct consequence of our failure as the governing party to ensure that we do not allow the *new normal* to emerge and take root.

It is vitally important that all our people, and the ANC first and foremost, must understand that the state capture, corruption and the other negatives I have mentioned would never have become entrenched determinants of the future of our country if the ANC had done the right thing – concretely, in action, to refuse to allow its ranks to be filled by people who do not share its fundamental values.

The recent, 2019, elections have confirmed the ANC as our country's governing party at the national level and in eight of our Provinces.

Given what I have said, it is obvious that unless what continues to be our governing party, the ANC, rids itself of those who join or remain in the organisation to abuse state power in their selfish interest, the conditions will remain for the continued perpetration of the crimes of state capture, corruption, and so on.

In this context, we must take very serious note of the allegations that have been made that many of the negative interventions made by the ANC or ANC members, owe their origin to *agents provocateurs*, and are counter-revolutionary in nature.

Allegedly, these *provocateurs* are agents who were infiltrated by the apartheid intelligence services into the ANC and other organisations of the democratic movement during the struggle years. It is believed that they are still ANC members and continue to be controlled by their erstwhile apartheid handlers. Thus they have not abandoned their strategic task of defeating the ANC and the democratic revolution!

The proposal is therefore made that an examination of the misdemeanours attributed to the ANC must include an investigation of whether these might have originated from the *agents provocateurs* I have mentioned, and are therefore part of the more radical attempt to achieve counter-revolutionary objectives.

Perhaps you are wondering what this, and my reference to the Judicial Commissions, has to do with this interesting and educative book, *Betting on a Darkie*.

The nature and calibre of ANC members is of strategic importance to the future of our country. To date, none of the political parties, nor the major observers and analysts, has questioned the perspective that the ANC will remain the dominant political force, even after 2019.

What I have said makes the plain and obvious statement that unless the ANC cleans up its membership to ensure that, at all levels, it is made up of people who respect its value system, and join and remain in the organisation with the sole purpose of serving the people of South Africa, our country will fail to wipe out the negative phenomena of counter-revolution, state capture, corruption and the other negatives that have preoccupied our Judicial Commissions of Inquiry.

This harks back to my assertion in 2000: that for it to serve the people of South Africa properly, the ANC has to develop its own members as 'cadres who are truly politically committed to the all-round success of the new democratic South Africa, and properly prepared with regard to the skills our country needs to achieve that success…'

Regrettably, our history since that statement was made has told the painful story that it is not easy to find such cadres in our country. Evidence presented at the Judicial Commissions of Inquiry to which I have referred, among others, speaks of people in the public and private sectors who have the requisite skills, but clearly are not committed to the all-round success of the new democratic South Africa.

These skilled cadres include politicians, public service, corporate and other managers, corporate owners and managers, accountants, lawyers, prosecutors, police officers, journalists, trade unionists, religious leaders, and others.

The urgent question is: where will South Africa find the development cadres it urgently requires?

I began my Foreword by saying I was pleased Nyati had decided to write this book and that Kwela Books had agreed to publish it. I wrote this after careful reading, from beginning to the end, of the manuscript.

This appropriately entitled book, *Betting on a Darkie*, tells the immensely empowering and energising real (rather than fictional) story that we *do* have in our country exactly the kind of cadres South Africa needs to extricate itself from its political, economic and social crisis.

This story shows us that, while we must listen with great

attention to, and act on, the depressing stories told at the Judicial Commissions, we must not lose sight of so much else in our country that is positive and exciting!

As told in *Betting on a Darkie*, that 'much else' in our country is about the progression of a black boy, Mteto Nyati, who grew up during the apartheid years in the stultifying rural Bantustans that colonialism and apartheid had imposed on the national majority, but who develops to become one of the giants in the world of global business – essentially a pioneer in successful business management, and therefore global wealth creation.

More than this, because Nyati developed into a professional with a vision greater than a mere focus on profit for the companies he led, and a fat salary and share options for himself, he has come to stand out as more than the modern successful business manager.

Betting on a Darkie has come exactly at the right time in the context of the historical evolution of our country. This is because it tells us of what is, in fact, an historic accomplishment. It says that what I stated in 2000 as an aspiration has, at least in part, been achieved.

Through this detailed, empowering and inspiring story, we see that our country has Nyati as a living and active example of the kind of development cadre South Africa requires: one who has the skills modern society needs and who is committed to building our country as a viable democracy.

He combines practical commitment to the *ubuntu* value system, commitment to selflessly serving the people, principled opposition to corruption and disadvantaging the disadvantaged, and developing his skills so he can use them to improve the life conditions of the masses of our people.

22

The public hearings at the Judicial Commissions have communicated the very disturbing message that for many years, the middle strata in our country, the professionals, have effectively betrayed the democratic revolution.

Objectively, it was expected that this democratic revolution would benefit those in the middle strata, materially and otherwise (as it did). It was also expected to improve the life conditions of the poor and disadvantaged through changes brought about by input from the middle strata in both the public and private sectors.

The preponderant message coming through during the public hearings of the Judicial Commissions is that those middle strata, the professionals, failed to do what was expected of them, especially relative to their own selfless professional conduct and their willingness to serve the interests of the poor and marginalised.

This book says that despite this, we must draw inspiration from the fact that out of sight of general public knowledge, we do indeed have members of the middle strata who have honestly and systematically discharged their responsibilities as selfless agents of change for the success of democratic South Africa.

It is in this context that I have called Nyati a role model – a role model in the context of the urgent and strategic task of ensuring that our country has a critical mass of middle-strata cadres who must honestly and selflessly play their role, as Nyati has.

I am privileged to strongly commend *Betting on a Darkie* to the South African reading public, hoping that we, the reading public, will impress on our government that it should study

Betting on a Darkie in order to empower itself to address the task of building cadres for development.

Let us use the example set by Nyati, with him involved, to educate our young people to aim to be our new Mteto Nyatis!

This book, *Betting on a Darkie*, must serve as one of our teaching instruments, an honest and informative tool to help us produce principled cadres modelled on Mteto Nyati. This will help our country to achieve the noble goal of a better life for all.

PRESIDENT THABO MBEKI – Johannesburg 2019

Preface

Dream your own dreams; achieve your own goals.
Your journey is your own and unique.
Roy T Bennett – The Light in the Heart

When I look back, I know with certainty there are many things I should not have done. But they are part of me, part of who I have become, and they have a place in the context of my life. They are reminders that mistakes can be built on, that journeys are filled with learning and that the right path, whatever 'right' may mean for you, is often only a step away.

My formative years were by my mother's side in a Transkei trading store, a business that supported her extended family and serviced a community. She shattered all stereotypes of a woman's place in the patriarchal Eastern Cape of the 1970s and '80s and taught her offspring that economic independence can liberate. The role my parents played in our lives is evident in the tributes from my brother and sister, included after the first chapter.

My career has been defined by challenges I approached with trepidation at first: from my first job in the '80s, trying to cope in a stiff-upper-lip environment where I felt a bit like one of the characters in *Hidden Figures*, to being tasked with developing a computerised decision support system when I'd barely operated a computer, to becoming a communications salesman for IBM when my training was that of a mechanical engineer. I learned that success lay in being myself and in retaining my status as an outsider. Try too hard to blend in and you may well disappear. At Afrox I was the only black engineer. When I arrived to take up a position with IBM in Paris in the early 2000s, there was no one like me. Colleagues were unsure of how to treat me – my differences made me stand out. I decided to use what set me apart to my advantage and to take on every challenge that came my way as if it were an engineering project. Later I began seeking out those challenges and relishing them, while also developing an awareness of my responsibility as a pathfinder. It was important to open opportunities, not only for myself, but for others too. Sometimes this rested heavily on my shoulders.

Although I am a product of my circumstances, I believe we carry knowledge within us from elsewhere, enabling us to make better choices in this life. If we get the right parents, as I did, these choices come easier. Inner knowing helped me choose the right mentors in the form of brave managers who took the risk of betting on a darkie in times when people like me weren't considered for thinking roles in business. Neil Greenfield, Mpho Letlape, Mark Harris, Ali Faramawy and Jean-Philippe Courtois showed leadership in their ability to place prejudice aside and to embrace diversity. Their gamble gave me the confidence to succeed and created an environment in which I gained courage to do things I wasn't sure I could. There are many others who have been part of my journey and, in line with my value of 'openness', I invited some of them to share their perspectives and insights. I believe their contributions greatly enrich the narrative of this book.

MTETO NYATI – Johannesburg, 2019

Chapter 1

The Shopkeeper's Son

Our character is not so much the product of race and heredity
as of those circumstances by which nature forms our habits,
by which we are nurtured and live.
          – Cicero

My father wanted me to be a doctor: of that he made
no secret. He planted the idea in my head, and anyone else's who
would listen, from when I was very young. He'd wanted to study
medicine, but in his day medical training for blacks was inferior
and he felt sure he'd end up as a glorified nurse, so he studied to
be a teacher instead.

Even long after I'd decided I wanted to study engineering,
Bhuti, as I called him because I'd grown up hearing my aunts
calling him that, didn't stop trying to change my mind. When,
in 1982, he drove me to Durban from Mthatha to start my first
year in the engineering faculty at Natal University (now the University
of KwaZulu-Natal), he pestered me all the way.

'Bhele, why don't you just do medicine?' was the intermittent
refrain for over 400 km.

What made him more adamant was that residences were
racially segregated and the only one that would accept black students
was the Alan Taylor Residence in Wentworth, which housed
medical students. In addition, the government of the then 'inde-

pendent' Transkei gave bursaries to students who chose medicine. Instead, he and my mother had to pay for my engineering studies and I had to find digs off campus. It just didn't make sense to him.

'Everything, Bhele, is pointing to medicine!'

In his mind, engineering was a bit like being a car mechanic: good for a hobby, but not for a career. However, my mother had watched me, as a curious child, dismantling her radio to see how it worked, fiddling with car engines and puzzling over why a paraffin fridge was cold if it had a flame. And she supported me.

'You do what you want, Dlambulo.'

When we got to Durban, my father drove straight to the medical school at King Edward VIII Hospital, hoping against hope that I would change my mind when I saw the place. There he met up with an old friend, a nursing sister, who agreed to provide me with accommodation in Umlazi. We dropped off my belongings at her home, but I didn't feel entirely comfortable with the arrangement.

While registering, I bumped into a school friend, Loyiso 'Blackie' Magqaza, who told me about prefab accommodation for black Howard College students living at Alan Taylor Residence (used by black medical students). I jumped at the chance of being spared the long commute to and from Umlazi.

I shared a dormitory with the likes of Thembani Bukula, Mce Booi, and Manderese Panyana. Many years later, when Thembani was energy regulator at NERSA, he and his team had to withstand unrelenting political pressure, either not to put up Eskom tariffs because it was election year, or to put them up in order to afford the nuclear deal. I felt proud of my former dorm mate, who always did what he believed was right.

Thankfully, for my father's sake, my brother Fundile, three years my junior, became a doctor. My sister Pelokazi studied physiotherapy and the last born, Langa, became an engineer like me.

Both my parents were teachers, trained under the Cape Education Department before Bantu education was introduced. They came from a long line of teachers – even my great-grandfather was in the profession. Bhuti taught Latin, English and History. He was a great raconteur and loved connecting history and religion to real life, be it sitting around with his friends drinking whisky, in the pulpit as a sub-deacon, as headmaster in front of his school, or as master of ceremonies at a community function. He particularly loved telling stories when he had a captive audience stuck in the car with him on a trip somewhere. One of his favourites was recounting how our ancestors had fled from the warriors of Sigidi kaSenzangakhona – King Shaka – in the Mfecane wars of the nineteenth century. When they reached the Eastern Cape, the Xhosas didn't accept them either. Various tribes, dispersed by the Zulu armies and shunned by the Xhosa, came together, forming the Fingo nation, a name referring to their status as wanderers, or displaced people. After years of oppression by the amaGcaleka in the Transkei, the Fingo established themselves in the south-western corner of what is now the Eastern Cape. In the 1830s they forged an alliance with English missionaries – considered one of the worst things black people could do at the time, as it meant declaring loyalty to the British and their god. But it was also a commitment to education.

And that shaped us.

My mother taught grades 1 and 2 at Ntlaza Junior Primary School in the Ngqeleni district where, because rules weren't always rules, I was allowed to attend classes from the age of four, instead of six. My brothers and sister did the same.

My mom also dabbled in raising poultry and pigs. My daily chore was to fetch leftover food from St Barnabas Hospital, about 2 km away, to feed the pigs. I was about eight years old and I'd set off at the crack of dawn, pushing a wheelbarrow. The driver of a bread delivery truck got so used to seeing me that he would hoot twice to greet me. I began looking forward to this sound as it was eerily quiet at 5 am and the road ahead seemed interminable. I had two older half-brothers and didn't understand why I was the only one doing hard labour. I even started believing I had been adopted and that my parents were making me do this because I was the outsider who needed to pay for his keep. But those solitary walks sculpted me; today I often prefer my own company and thoughts.

When I was in standard 2 (grade 4) Theophilus Mvelase Mbambisa, an education inspector, asked my father to start a secondary school at Tabase, about 60 km away from where we lived. For some reason my father hero-worshipped Mr Mbambisa, calling him *mkhuluwa* – big brother. I suspect it was because his eldest son, Zwelidumile, was a medical doctor. Bhuti always had a soft spot for doctors.

The Transkei government had built a new junior school in Tabase. So we traded our comfortable brick home at Ntlaza, which had carpets on the floor and a tank for water, to live in the old mud school with cow-dung floors. We had to fetch water from a nearby river, so my sisters had to carry buckets of water on their heads, which they weren't used to. Instead of our old Dover wood stove, we had to use a primus, both for cooking and to boil water for bathing in a metal tub. Because there was no infrastructure in the area and the nearest store was 10 km away, my mother converted one of the old classrooms into a general dealer store by putting in double doors, burglar bars, and an L-shaped counter made of glass so that customers could see what was on offer. Later, she introduced clothing, bought wholesale from Sparg's in Mthatha. She cashed in her Bantu Education pension, bought a cream Toyota Hilux single cab, which had a bench seat, and loaded it with stock in Mthatha. The need was great and the business grew so quickly that my parents negotiated with the local chief, Inkosi Jumba, for land to build a bigger shop and a proper house. The shop came first, the house later. The community was a bit horrified when my father built us a temporary home of mud, branches and broken bricks.

But within two years we had a proper home and ran a well-equipped general dealer not far from the school where my father was headmaster. He had six children from a previous marriage who lived with us. Naturally it caused friction at times. Despite being a headmaster, he wasn't much of a disciplinarian at home. He always tried to be Mr Nice Guy, which made things difficult for my mother, who was strict with her own offspring, so faced being labelled the mean stepmother.

On the plus side, there were plenty of us to help out in the shop. My oldest half-brother and I would wake at half past four every second morning to do the bread-and-milk run to Mthatha. We'd be back by seven-thirty, in time to have a quick breakfast before school began at eight. My brother, who was six years older than me, didn't have a driver's licence, but we'd all learned to drive sitting on a pillow so we could see over the dashboard. My father was fussy about the Hilux. The Nyati sons should not leave home in a dusty vehicle, so he would make us wash it before we set off, even though we had miles of dirt roads ahead. There was a rumour that the national road between Engcobo and Mthatha was untarred because the construction company had pulled out of the area after one of the foremen was killed and eaten!

In Mthatha we'd collect the village mail from the post office, buy six dozen loaves of bread, go to the fresh produce market for fruit and vegetables, then to the dairy where we'd get big cans of milk – to be dispensed into customers' containers. By then, the Hilux, which had a canopy, was packed to the roof. On the drive home we'd breathe in the heavenly smell of freshly baked bread, which we'd sell in quarters at the shop for five cents each.

The shop gave us a sense of belonging in the community and a position in society. There was a kind of status that went with trading and I enjoyed interacting with customers. I would often advise them about new products – how, for example, they could use Compral painkillers instead of Panado. Many would arrive with a long shopping list and put their feet up while I found all the items they needed and entered them in our credit book. As their husbands were away working, many women could pay only when the men came home or sent money once a quarter. My mother made *magwinyas* and I'd take a bag of them to school, the aroma of fried dough pervading the classroom until the bell rang, making everyone's mouth water. When breaktime came these vetkoek didn't last long and I'd go home with a pocketful of jingling coins, which I handed over to my mother, who would count every cent.

The shop was close to the clinic, so it attracted passing trade. It was also a good place to meet girls: in the late afternoon, young people would gather outside the shop, sit on paraffin tins and play *ama*dice and cards for money. I loved the thrill of this amateur gambling and longed to join in. But my mother had other plans for me. While my classmates played, I'd be doing chores. We had an old-fashioned scale in the shop and I would make up 500 g, 1 kg and 2 kg bags of onions, potatoes and carrots from the veg-etables we'd bought at the fresh produce market in Mthatha. I'd get the exact weight by putting the vegetables on the scale, then adding cast-iron weights to the other side until the scale balanced. Then I'd pop the veggies into plastic bags and price them with a koki pen. I would sort the mail and sometimes read letters for illiterate customers. In the process I'd sometimes hear stuff that wasn't for pre-teen ears, such as details about family dramas or even illegitimate children.

We were the first to get a landline telephone in the area, which changed the life of a community whose relatives were migrant workers in Johannesburg and other far-flung places. Being able to verbally communicate with them made distances shorter. Our phone number was 'Tabase 6'. I'd crank the handle to get hold of the central exchange and an old lady waiting next to me would bellow out the number she needed. It took all of them a while to realise that they didn't have to shout, merely talk into the phone, but eventually they got it. When the phone rang, my siblings or I would rush off to find whoever the call was for, while the caller hung on for minutes on end.

Real progress came when my mother bought a diesel generator. It made a huge noise, but our neighbours tolerated it because of the advantages that came with it: trading hours were extended until after dark, food and drinks were kept cold and we also ran a freezer for ice and meat. The arrival of an electronic cash register meant that we didn't have to count bank bags of coins every night. My eyes lit up almost as brightly as the numbers on the screen when I saw it magically come to life for the first time.

To my mother, nothing was impossible. She was the only woman in the area with a Code 10 (heavy duty) driver's licence and her actions sent a message to others in the community: don't wait for things to come to you. Eventually the shop did so well and expanded so much that she took on some employees, bought a Mazda truck and hired a driver. The shop was called Embekweni Store – place where you are respected – and my mother's name was Nombeko – the one who has respect, which was how she treated everyone who worked for her. This has stayed with me and influenced me: treat people properly and they'll respect you.

Having helpers in the shop meant that I had time to hang out with my friends. I didn't always use my new-found time well. At the end of my primary-school years, my mother – despite her busy life – began noticing that I often smelled like petrol. This was because my friends and I stole petrol meant for our vehicles and inhaled it to get high. It took her a while to confront me, but when she did she lost it good and proper, beating me with a stick. This, in addition to my brother having told on me for smoking second-hand cigarette stompies, was enough to make my parents decide to pack me off to boarding school. It was non-negotiable. Bhuti said nothing, just looked on as my mother sat me down and told me I was to begin grade 8 at St Patrick's Mission in Libode, almost 50 km from home.

It seemed to me a lonely prison without my large extended family and the hustle and bustle of the shop. The teachers were Catholic nuns whose only priorities were discipline, education and prayer. From the moment I set eyes on her, I was terrified of Sister Principal, the headmistress. Three times a day the Angelus bell would ring and we had to stop whatever we were doing and pray:

> Hail Mary full of Grace, the Lord is with thee . . . Holy Mary, Mother of God, pray for us sinners now and at the hour of our death. Amen.

Apart from our lessons, we had to work in the vegetable gardens and grow our own food, which I thought they cooked really badly. I was used to better. My consolation was a tin trunk filled with goodies from home, which I tucked into on Sundays when no one was looking. My treat times ended when some older boys discovered my secret stash, broke the lock of my trunk and took everything. I never said a word, just watched them with a lump in my throat as they relished my cans of pilchards and my biscuits.

St Patrick's Mission drew learners from far and wide. I shared a bunk bed with a boy named Lizo Mbetshu from New Brighton, Port Elizabeth. Today he's an ophthalmologist in East London. I met other boys from Cape Town, Durban and Joburg who re-layed stories about 'black power' riots in their townships. They talked about police brutality and tear gas. I found these stories of state violence hard to believe. Nationally, resistance against oppressive education policies was at boiling point. It was 1976. Back in Tabase, my father was organising learners to protect his school from protestors. The Transkei government had fuelled the narrative that uneducated 'influences' from Soweto would arrive to disrupt learning in the homeland, and my father believed this.

I remained focused on my studies and gradually my grades improved. I came to love science and maths and I was sporty, having inherited a love of rugby from my father, who'd introduced it at all the schools he'd taught at. I continued playing rugby at university – first as scrumhalf, then wing – until I broke my collarbone in a bruising match against the University of Zululand.

I also enjoyed soccer and because I was quick, with loads of energy, at school they nicknamed me 'double engine' until I somehow burst the only soccer ball we had and I was called much ruder names.

In 1978, I began my high school at St John's College in Mthatha, one of the oldest schools in the country and the most prestigious in Transkei. You'd find a lot of black parents from all over the country sending their kids to St John's.

The school logo has an eagle holding a Bible, with the motto 'Rise like an eagle and shine like a star'. I decided that's what I needed to do.

In their desire to make sure we were properly educated, my parents had no qualms about sending us to a mission school, which meant that we had to be boarders. People in Tabase didn't understand why anyone would want to send their children away to be influenced by others: the fear was that they might not want to do physical labour after being cosseted. Although St John's – founded as a theological college by missionary Bishop Henry Callaway in 1879 – shied away from political involvement, the school system was firmly based on the principles of equality. Our teachers came from all walks of life and from all over the world. They had a liberal outlook and wanted to make a difference in a sea of injustice.

In 1978 Vuyisile 'PV' Maneli took over as principal and became the first black head of St John's. He was a talented rugby player – he'd been a member of the Leopards team, also known as the African XV – and had studied maths and science in the US during the '60s. At last I had a role model who looked like me. He encouraged us to compete against each other for good grades, to choose an area of expertise and excel at it.

Each year the school competed in the International Science Olympiad (ISO). The aim of the competition was to promote careers in science, pit the brightest students in the world against one another and to compare teaching systems in different countries. Doing well in an ISO virtually guaranteed you university entrance and a bursary from Anglo American.

In my first year at St John's, when I was in grade 10, a grade 12 learner named Derek Hughes was selected to represent South Africa at the ISO. I looked up to Derek, who was the goalkeeper for the school soccer team. When he told me about an academic scholarship available to top grade 10 students, I set my mind to it. I was awarded a full scholarship, which brought some financial relief for my parents who were raising ten children.

In 1980, I was the top student and I was chosen to represent South Africa at the ISO (International Science Olympiad) in

London. Derek had taught me how to act on my dreams. It was a big deal at St John's and before I left I had to make a speech in front of everyone, including officials from the Education Department. As I wasn't much of an orator, a more outspoken friend, Oyama Mabandla, decided this was a good opportunity to put words in my mouth. He wrote me a speech that any revolutionary would've been proud of. It surprised my classmates and teachers, coming from someone who didn't usually express strong political opinions.

My parents had never been abroad, nor had anyone in Tabase, and I had never travelled beyond the borders of Transkei. At just sixteen years old, I flew to Joburg to be put through my paces at an orientation week sponsored by Anglo American. Sister Lane, who had succeeded Maneli as school principal, organised for the entire grade 12 contingent to be at Mthatha's KD Matanzima Airport to see me off.

In Joburg white students were taught to sing 'Nkosi Sikelel' iAfrika', black students to sing 'Die Stem', and how to use a knife and fork – a rather telling assumption that we didn't know how.

The visit to London exposed me to a world I'd never considered and, after a fortnight, I returned home as Tabase's expert in international affairs and post-matric careers.

The *Daily Dispatch* newspaper published an article on me, no doubt egged on by my father, who said I had plans to study medicine the following year. What he didn't know was that my mind was set on mechanical engineering – nothing else.

For my first year I enrolled for a Bachelor of Science degree at the University of Transkei (Unitra), which didn't offer engineering. Black students had to get permission from the Ministry of

Higher Education if they wanted to study engineering. When he was the minister of native affairs, HF Verwoerd – the so-called architect of apartheid – had said something like: 'What is the use of teaching a Bantu child mathematics when he cannot use it in practice?'

At Unitra I reconnected with former classmates such as Andile Mvinjelwa and Zwai Tshwele. I did well; my only real competition came from a student named Xoliswa Kakana, who had done her matric at Inanda High School in Durban. She qualified in Germany as an electronics engineer and became the founder, chairperson and group CEO of ICT-Works.

A curious thing happened on my first day at Unitra. I was about to get into a lift on campus when I spotted an envelope on the floor and picked it up. It was full of banknotes, enough for tuition and accommodation for the whole year. There was no one around. For a moment I panicked. What should I do? I got into the lift and pressed the button to close the door.

I kept the envelope, waiting to hear if anyone had lost money. Eventually I used it to pay what my parents owed the university. When I told my mother about it she decided it must have been God smiling on us. Did I make the right decision? Maybe I should have done things differently and handed it in. But I didn't.

For my second year I applied to the University of Natal's engineering faculty. Even though I had won the science olympiad, I still had to apply for ministerial permission. But the university refused to accept my first year BSc credits from Unitra. I had to do physics, applied maths and chemistry all over again. It worked to my advantage because I was a novice at two of my other subjects: engineering drawing and design, and calculus.

Calculus and engineering drawing were part of the matric syllabus at white schools but weren't in the Bantu Education curriculum, maths included only algebra, geometry and trigonometry. Black engineering students were at a distinct disadvantage. Dissecting a piston engine in your mind is one thing, being expected to draw it from memory was another. A number of dreams were shattered, as calculus, drawing and design effectively became a tool to exclude black students from the faculty of engineering. The playing fields were not level.

In 1989, the Council for Scientific and Industrial Research (CSIR) calculated that of the 163 800 professionals working in the fields of science and technology, just one per cent were black.

In lectures, I found myself a seat at the front of the class, constantly asked questions and concentrated on my drawing and design, assured of cruising through my other subjects, second time round. Just three black mechanical engineering students made it to second year: me, Edwin Mabelane and Joe Mathebula. Edwin became a GM at Eskom and he and I would meet up in later years in rather different circumstances.

My stint at Natal University politicised me and I joined the Azanian Students' Organisation (AZASO). Its leaders were Joe Phaahla, now deputy health minister and Aaron Motsoaledi, the current home affairs minister. Others I came into contact with were ANC heavyweights Zweli Mkhize and Siyabonga Cwele, former KZN health MEC Sibongiseni Dhlomo and Dr Judy Dlamini, chancellor of Wits University.

Through friends from St John's such as Oyama Mabandla and Mce Booi, whose father had been a minister in the Transkei government, I became active in the ANC's underground network.

Both eventually went into exile – Oyama to Lesotho where he helped set up MK cells, linking operatives to units based in Transkei and the Eastern Cape and recruiting people for missions. We would travel to Lesotho for weekends, on the pretext of attending graduation ceremonies at Roma University in Maseru. The contacts I made led to many unexpected overnight visitors to my university room – activists who were passing through on some or other operation, the details of which I never found out.

When the United Democratic Front (UDF) was launched in Cape Town on 20 August 1983, the AZASO hired a bus and we travelled down to draw courage from the likes of Joe Marks, Frank Chikane, Archie Gumede, Helen Joseph, Popo Molefe, Frances Baard and Pius Langa. I was nineteen years old and was inspired by the defiant mood – freedom now! The powerful gathering in Mitchells Plain was peaceful though, and I felt part of a momentous event. I was particularly impressed with Dr Allan Boesak, and judged him to be a great orator:

> [T]he formation of the United Democratic Front . . . symbolises the crisis apartheid and its supporters have created for themselves. After a history of some 331 years of slavery, racial discrimination, dehumanisation and economic exploitation, what they expected were acceptance of the status quo, docility and subservience.
>
> Instead they are finding a people, refusing to accept racial injustice and ready to face the challenges of the moment . . .
>
> After more than twenty years of apartheid education they expected to see totally brainwashed, perfect little 'hotnotjies'

and 'kaffirtjies' who knew their place in the world. Instead, they find the most politically conscious generation of young people determined to struggle for a better future.

He reminded us that one of the reasons the UDF was formed was to fight the introduction of the farcical Tricameral Parliament, intended to further entrench the exclusion of the black population, designated to homelands:

> So our African brothers and sisters will be driven even further into the wilderness of homeland politics, millions will have to find their political rights in the sham independence of those bush republics; millions more will be forcibly removed from their homes into resettlement camps.
>
> Clearly the oppression will continue, the brutal break-up of black family life will not end. The apartheid line is not all abolished, it is simply shifted so as to include those so-called coloureds and Indians who are willing to co-operate with the government.

We returned to Natal invigorated into supporting the UDF's Million Signatures Campaign and went round canvassing in Wentworth, a semi-industrial area of Durban to which coloured people had been relocated.

Despite my extramural activities, I didn't neglect my studies.

I was the only black engineering student to graduate in my year, others having fallen victim to engineering drawing and design, calculus – or politics, never far from the life of a black student.

After my final year exams, I went back to Tabase, where I found my mother hosting a group of MK activists who had come to see me. One of them was a former St John's classmate from Alice who had been politically active against the repressive homeland governments and had skipped the country. Now he was back and in my family home; Transkei was an important infiltration route for MK activists.

This group was on what appeared to be an operation of some sort. I found myself eyeing their many bags anxiously, wondering if they contained weapons. Up until then my involvement in the struggle had been mainly on an intellectual level. I didn't know what their mission was – nor was I sure that they did. One Saturday night I took them partying in Southernwood, Mthatha, near Unitra. At some point during the evening, one of my mysterious guests came and told me he had 'lost a hand grenade'. We set about hunting for the missing device and attracting unnecessary attention, I thought. It seemed to me a rather haphazard operation and it was with sadness, but not surprise, that I heard some months later that the group had been ambushed and killed by police near Fort Jackson in East London.

*

At the end of my first semester at Natal University, Afrox – a subsidiary of a British industrial gas company called BOC (of which I had never heard) – gave me a bursary to complete my degree. Then, in my final year, I was offered a Rhodes scholarship to study towards a master's degree in engineering in Germany. It would have taken me away from South Africa for two years. I turned it down because, at the time, my mother wasn't in good health: she had debilitating stomach pains that doctors couldn't attribute to anything in particular. She, however, kept sending out signals that she wasn't long for this world. It was probably overwork and stress, but I didn't feel comfortable moving so far away from her.

It was the right decision. I was destined for business, not academia.

I headed for Selby, Joburg, the headquarters of Afrox.

Our Nyati family as we know it today are descendants of the Fingo people of the Eastern Cape, refugees from the 'Shaka Wars' (1818–1828) in KwaZulu-Natal. They were allocated land in the 'buffer zone' between the 1820 settlers of Grahamstown and the indigenous Xhosa people of the Far Eastern Cape.

These destitute Fingos were then caught up in the Frontier Wars between the Xhosas and the settlers. Although they tried to integrate with the indigenous Xhosa communities, they were not fully accepted.

On 14 May 1835, our Fingo forefathers gathered under a milkwood tree in the Peddie district, in the presence of a missionary, Reverend John Ayliff, who was sympathetic to their refugee status. At that gathering they swore a Great Oath ('Fingo Oath') that:

They would obey the Queen of England;

They would accept Christianity; and

They would educate their children.

Because of their alliance with the colonial forces, the Fingos were the first African people to use ploughs and to plant wheat. They were well educated and secured the bulk of elite positions as clerks, teachers and traders.

As descendants of the Fingo people, in line with the 'Fingo Oath', our family valued education more than anything. It was a practical route to a better life. We've passed on the Fingo education gene – my son is an engineering graduate from MIT in Massachusetts and Mteto's daughter, Anda, is a pre-medical student in Baltimore.

Our dad, Michael Mtutuzeli Nyati, born in 1929, became a teacher, like his parents and grandparents before him. But what he really wanted was to be a medical doctor. He matriculated from Healdtown College in 1947 as top student in the Cape Province. Before that, he had been the best student at St John's College in Mthatha, where he obtained his Junior Certificate.

My siblings and I followed in his footsteps and also went to St John's and did well enough to obtain merit bursaries.

In 1948, when apartheid was enacted, our dad was among the first group of 'medical' students at the newly opened Medical School for blacks at Wentworth, outside Durban.

A year into the programme, he was expelled. Black students had discovered that they weren't actually being trained as doctors and revolted. They were being trained as auxiliaries, professional nurses, only good enough to assist white doctors. As one of the protest leaders, my dad was kicked out of Wentworth and forced to go back to Transkei, where he grudgingly took up the tried-and-tested family profession.

He obtained his Bachelor of Arts degree from the University of South Africa through correspondence.

Although he became a headmaster, his dream of being a doctor never died, and he tried to make it live on in his children. I am the only one who bit and he was proud of that.

Our dad got married when he was only 23 years old. He had five children with his first wife (three girls and two boys), and also had an extramarital girl child. When they divorced, he obtained custody of all his kids.

In 1963, he met our mom Nombeko Annie Nogemane. They married and had four children, three boys and a girl. The oldest of the kids from the second marriage was a boy named Mteto Silumko Mzuvukile, born on 21 December 1964; followed by me, Fundile Mabhelandile three years later, and then Pelokazi Nomfundo in August 1968. The last-born, in 1970, was Mcebisi Langa, on our mom's birthday, 14 April.

When my mom married our dad, she took on a lot more than a husband. She had to play a parenting role to six stepchildren, and later to her own four children. Two parents and ten kids in one household! In her attempts to ensure that she would not be perceived as soft on her biological kids, she was big on discipline. My mom was of the belief that sparing the rod would spoil the child. Even the name Mteto means law, order, discipline.

When my mother decided to quit teaching in the mid-'70s to run our store in the Tabase Mission village, she expected Mteto to spend his free time assisting at the shop. So he grew up behind the counter of a general dealer, serving rural customers, and respecting them. Growing up with a businesswoman – and the only woman who drove a truck in Mthatha – taught us that success does not come easily, and that women are as good as men, if not better.

As firstborn, Mteto had it tough sometimes, especially when he began to be naughty in his early teens. Despite her heavy hand, our mom loved Mteto so much and shaped him into something the rest of us could follow. She was determined, in bringing him up, that he would be a role model and useful member of society.

He was our mom's 'guinea pig' – she tried to create a child who would not take privilege for granted, a child who could put himself in the shoes of others, a child who valued focus and hard work as the only way to sustainable success, a child who would lead others without making them feel small.

Mteto has always been an inspiration, but there are a few things I would not ask his advice on: the latest fashion, parties or music. I would not go to him at all. He is slow in those areas . . . he prefers sitting at home reading biographies and motivational books, or travelling the world.

– Dr Fundile Nyati is CEO of Proactive Health Solutions

Bhuti Mteto was always my hero: from the first memory I have of him, which goes back to the age of three. He would act like a 'mother hen', fending off anything, or anyone that threatened my wellbeing. I would run to him crying and he would tell me to be brave like a boy and make me confront the bullies. It made me fearless, which didn't always work in my favour. In my teenage years, most boys were scared of me because I would intimidate them. Bhuti Mteto would even confront our mom, telling her not to raise her voice at 'the child' (me) because she would make me nervous. He was my protector and my hero.

When Mteto went overseas as part of the Youth Science Olympiad, I was scared that he would never return because no one in my family had ever gone abroad. When he did, he brought me a miniature of London's Tower Bridge. It ignited my passion for overseas travel.

I doubt that he will like my reference to the fact that in higher primary he sang so sweetly that he was placed with the female voices in the school choir. We teased him.

Because of the standards he set at school, our mom and dad expected nothing less from us and at times it made life difficult. He always excelled, setting the bar very high for his younger siblings. In my first year at St John's College, the teachers told me in no uncertain terms that as Mteto and Fundile's younger sister, I was expected to achieve excellent grades. The pressure helped mould achievers in our family.

In his university years, Mteto and his friends listened to Radio Freedom and his political icon was former president Thabo Mbeki. I used to fear that Mteto would get detained, or disappear like other student activists. Although he didn't realise it, he was a big influence on my political activism when I got to university. I did not listen to anyone who held views that differed from his.

The quest for academic excellence our parents instilled in us fuelled the work ethic we all have today and within all of us is a streak of business leadership, which we learned from our mother. I could never trade this for anything.

– Pelokazi Madlingozi is an Executive Manager at
Proactive Health Solutions

Chapter 2

Johannesburg 1986

Circumstances are beyond human control, but our conduct is within our power.
— Benjamin Disraeli

My previous experience of the City of Gold had been as a cosseted sixteen-year-old science olympiad student. As an adult, I found it somewhat daunting and I became aware, more than ever, of the many sides to South Africa. Afrox head office, where I was to undergo a training period, was in Selby, near the city centre. Blacks weren't allowed to live there so I had to find a place in Soweto, which was the closest township – about an hour's ride away on public transport. I'd never stayed in a densely populated area before, let alone in one that was a hot-bed of political activity. A protest campaign, which took on various forms, was gaining momentum across the country: in Soweto there were rent boycotts, mass stayaways and a spirit of defiance that even a constant military and police presence couldn't dampen. In the city and surrounds there were occasional bomb blasts at railway stations, police stations, hotels and shopping centres.

I put my head down and concentrated on my new job. Afrox had invested in me, paying my fees from the second semester of my first year for the duration of my four-year degree. A condition of my scholarship was that during my university holidays I had to work at Afrox air-separation plants. My first job had been at a gas plant at Maydon Wharf in Durban, where I was issued with company overalls, gloves and boots and assigned to a boilermaker, who taught me how to weld. If my father had seen me – as a boilermaker's gopher – his preconceived ideas about engineers would've been justified. Later, through guided experiments, I learned to research methods to improve oxygen yields from air. Gases such as oxygen, nitrogen, helium and argon are present in the air. Through cooling them past their boiling point, they are separated into components, transforming them into liquid oxygen and nitrogen – required for Afrox's production needs. It was my first stab at chemical engineering.

The only person I knew at Afrox HQ was the labour relations manager, Lot Ndlovu, who had recruited me. He was an industrial relations expert whose ability to sidestep unions in favour of workplace forums made him useful to Afrox. Under him, grievances never made it beyond the factory floor. Cosatu had been launched in 1985 and its programme of 'rolling mass action' unnerved many in white-run industries. In the '90s Lot would become president of the Black Management Forum (BMF), CEO of People's Bank and a proponent of the reversal of inequality through realistic negotiated targets – Black Economic Empowerment.

But in the '80s, black corporate professionals were limited to a few experiments like me. It was tough. Lot's only advice to me was 'don't mess up'.

With his help I found a place to stay in Diepkloof – an electrified, fairly modern two-bedroomed house I shared with a guy from Limpopo. My housemate John and I took turns to do the cooking; he produced pap and I made *umngqusho onembotyi* (samp and beans). The rent was R200 a month, my salary R2 500, so I had enough left over to send money home. My three siblings still had to get through university; my mother wasn't as strong as she used to be and business-wise there was competition in Tabase as other trading stores had opened up.

There was a bus stop a few kilometres from my new Soweto home and I caught a Putco bus to work every morning. I wasn't exactly the epitome of sartorial elegance. I didn't own a suit and wore the same jacket and tie every day, with mismatched trousers and shirts.

Afrox abided by the Sullivan principles, developed by African American preacher, Reverend Leon Sullivan. He'd been on the board of General Motors in the US during the '70s and had used his corporate foothold to act against apartheid. General Motors was the biggest employer of black workers in South Africa at the time and, through pressure from Sullivan, had adopted a code of conduct that promoted corporate social responsibility and non-discrimination in the workplace. It encouraged other companies to do the same. So when I got to work at Afrox, segregation was temporarily suspended and I could use the bathroom, canteen and other facilities alongside white colleagues.

But I was still the elephant in the office. I was the only black engineer and the first black person ever to have been awarded a bursary. Apart from Lot Ndlovu, who was on another level, the only other black employees were cleaning and support staff. Not only did I have to make sure I didn't 'mess up', I would have to be the elephant that danced.

I became conscious that I – along with fellow bursary student Ruth Stenhouse, a Wits Chemical Engineering graduate – was an experiment. Afrox's internal newsletter, *Inform*, featured Ruth and me smiling broadly with our mentor, Dave Bawden, the operation engineer gases:

> As Afrox prepares for the future so its manning patterns, as with its technology, must mirror a changing world. The selection of Ruth Stenhouse and Mteto Nyati as Afrox bursars and then engineers-in-training gives an indication of the staff who will provide our technical expertise and leadership in the years ahead.
>
> Both these young graduates are members of minority groups: Ruth was one of three woman graduates in her class, Mteto, the only black graduate in his.
>
> When questioned about being the first woman engineer at Afrox, Ruth, in her practical and forthright way, said she believed it was an advantage. 'People are not likely to forget you,' she said.
>
> Mteto came to engineering along a traditional route; the mechanical fascination of repairing old cars told him where his interests and aptitudes lay.

Ruth and I, the rookies, were sent off to Afrox plants in Germiston and in Brits, the domain of the white male. I was pleased to have her with me. The looks we got and our exclusion from certain conversations made us acutely aware that we had to shatter stereotypes. I knew there was only one way to do this: by making myself useful.

My chance came when I was tasked with production planning at plants by monitoring customer demands. At the time, there was no system in place to accurately work out storage capacity and daily production, and no one seemed to even know if we should be generating more or less. I wasn't entirely sure how they expected me to work this out without data, and fleetingly wondered if they were just trying to keep me busy – or set me up for failure.

I didn't know where to start. Nothing in my degree had trained me for this, except for a brief introduction to computers in my fourth year, which I hadn't imagined would ever be of relevance to a career in engineering. I was familiar with a program called Fortran, a system developed by IBM in the '50s, which had evolved into an effective tool for numeric and scientific computing. Through working with it, I'd learned a set of computer instructions that could be used in different combinations to get the computer to produce specific outputs. Once I'd got the hang of it I was surprised how it helped me to think logically in life, but Fortran was far removed from the dBase III program I now had to get to grips with. dBase III had a completely different set of instructions: it was like learning a new language. There was no one who seemed willing or able to help me, so I started training myself.

I was given a laptop, a clunky white machine with a small screen in a clamshell-type cover, and began visiting plants to collect data. I gradually got caught up in programming, working out daily production, overtime needs and how to reduce costs. Within a year I had developed a 'prod-planning' monitoring module that matched required levels of production to resources, and estimated future demands.

I also helped put in place a system to make the delivery of our product more efficient. In those pre-GPS days, our drivers would be given their daily orders and disappear with their gas-laden tanks. Routes and distances weren't worked out or monitored, and drivers did their own thing, without accounting for their time or reporting what percentage of their schedules was taken up by deviations and breakdowns. I began accompanying them on their routes, calculating distances between deliveries. I spoke to sales agents, found out their needs, took into account customer complaints and came up with a computer program that streamlined the delivery process. It didn't sit too well with drivers who could no longer skive off once their deliveries were done, but it gave management a far better understanding of the company's operations.

Although I kept myself busy, I still couldn't shake off the feeling that I didn't fit, that I was being avoided instead of embraced. Once I'd finished a project, my next wasn't always waiting for me, despite the fact that Afrox was forging ahead, investing in healthcare and supplying oxygen to hospital groups, and trying to stay ahead of competitors such as Air Liquide and Air Products.

One of the managers, Neil Greenfield, had been sent overseas to find out about trends in Japan, which was in the midst of a three-decade-long economic miracle and way ahead of the pack in the field of technology. He reported back that the new world focus was on training and retraining employees in how to communicate with customers, to exceed customer expectations and how to use IT to improve customer satisfaction.

Neil was given funding to start a quality management unit. He selected me to be part of his four-man team. Under his guidance we were to develop an advanced trouble-shooting system that would ensure products and services were consistent and, if there was a problem, to be able to trace the source. In this way, customer needs were anticipated, complaints circumvented and management decisions based on evidence. One of our inventions, which I'm pleased to say is still around today, is the simple plastic seal on the neck of a gas bottle that traces its origins and production history.

I started realising the importance of teamwork and communication and finally felt as if I fitted in, that I wasn't a special case, an anomaly that needed to be kept busy. Neil, I rightly assumed, had chosen me because I had the necessary training to do what was expected of me. He became my mentor and under him I began approaching my job in a more methodical and professional way. He was about five years older than me and I admired that he seemed to have his life mapped out, planning to retire at 50 and travel the world, seeking places and adventures that challenged him.

Years later, when he was living in Germany and I was MD of Microsoft South Africa, we met up in Joburg. He had done as he'd said he would: given up formal work to explore the exotic and the unusual.

I thanked him for embracing diversity and for taking a bet on me.

One of my abiding memories of my work at Afrox in the 1980s is of us trainees in our overalls in the middle of a cold Highveld winter, getting workshop experience with the artisans at the Germiston plant. I used to think: did I really spend four years at university to dress like this and learn how to use a lathe? At first they taught us to use the workshop equipment and finally do a trade test, which meant following technical instructions and setting up the machines correctly, then it got more rigorous: working shifts and preparing for a shutdown. I remember being on duty from the Thursday before Good Friday and all the way through the Easter weekend – with minimal sleep.

I wasn't too intimidated by the all-white macho male atmosphere. My father was an artisan so I guess I was used to it, although working at the Germiston plant had its moments. The maintenance superintendent had wall-to-wall *Scope* centrefolds pinned up in his office! Mteto and I were definitely an anomaly: the regular staff weren't used to female or black trainees. I remember being sent to a steel foundry in Vereeniging and they wouldn't let us in, not believing that we were actually engineers. Mteto was always quiet and unchallenging, despite the patronising atmosphere at times. I was the only female to finish in my class at Wits and he the only black graduate in his at Natal, so we knew we'd be entering an environment where we stood out.

At our headquarters, just off the M2 in Selby, we had an office on the first floor and were under the wing of Dave Bawden. He was an operations engineer, but also mentored the new recruits. His main concern was that we keep our desks tidy! Cluttered desk, cluttered mind and all that . . .

Afrox human resources (HR) was fantastic – they would throw you in the deep end and then support you with training and good advice. There were lots of industrial strikes in the '80s so we had to do our heavy-duty driver's licence – Code 14 – and at one stage I drove oxygen trucks to hospitals at six in the morning. Talk about varied training.

Afrox HR set the tone for all my other jobs. I went from gas to drugs to alcohol! After Afrox I got a job with Adcock Ingram as logistics manager, then at SA Breweries as a project consultant, until they were taken over by AB InBev.

These days I design beer breweries all over the world – Tanzania, Romania, Canada – from my little office in Sandton. A few years ago I attended a project management course and the course leader, Amanda Ellis, had worked at Microsoft with Mteto and raved about his leadership and quoted him a lot. It took me back 30 years to that quiet trainee engineer who observed much and said little.

– Ruth Stenhouse Smith is senior design manager at
Blue Projects Company

Chapter 3

Choices and Consequences

*If you always do what you've always done, you'll always get
what you've always got.*   — *Anonymous*

Change was in the air. The unbanning of the ANC on
2 February 1990 was to open up a world of possibilities. The
Group Areas and Separate Amenities Acts were being eroded
and legislation changes meant that blacks could emerge from
the shadows. Anglo American had set the trend by buying up
property for its workers in Braamfontein and Hillbrow. All-white
blocks rapidly transformed into all-black blocks. I moved from
Soweto to Hillbrow to share a flat with an old school friend,
Hale Qangule, who had just finished studying at Wits. We lived
at Highpoint, a 28-floor apartment block, and led a sociable life.

I had a girlfriend back in Mthatha. I bought my first car, a
Toyota Conquest RSI, and would think nothing of leaving on a
Friday after work and travelling ten hours to Transkei for the
weekend, often with a carload of friends.

My weekend jaunts came to a temporary halt when, on my way
back to Joburg one Sunday morning, I collided with a truck re-
versing up a hill in my lane, near Qumbu. The errant truck
driver was injured when his face smashed into his steering wheel

and, although I didn't have a scratch on me, my car was a write-off. If the truck had been higher, it would have sliced off the roof and probably my head too. I'd been driving in convoy with a friend, Zwai Tshwele. When he realised that my car was a write-off, he drove me back to Tabase without hesitation, even though he needed to get back to work. Sometimes even the big-city rat race doesn't erase the concept of *ubuntu* – I am because you are.

I'd been driving too fast, but I did have my seat belt on. The incident changed my driving habits. Now I stick to the speed limit – particularly on mountain passes.

Sharing accommodation with Hale at Highpoint ended when I moved to Afrox's Pretoria West branch and became the engineer for the Northern Transvaal region and Swaziland. Downtown Pretoria was still very conservative, so I lived temporarily with a friend, Bonakele Qabaka, at his Waterkloof house. He was a diplomat, representing the government of the 'independent' Ciskei Bantustan. After two months there, I moved in with a colleague and his mother in Atteridgeville, where everyone spoke Sotho, except for me – or so it seemed. Reggie's mother was the sweetest person – most of the time – but she enjoyed her beer. After a drink or two, her hatred and mistrust of Xhosas became very evident. In my mind, tribalism and racism are one and the same. So it wasn't a happy time for me: at work I was surrounded by Afrikaans, at home by a part-time Xhosa hater. I tried to get away at weekends with a circle of friends who were studying at Wits.

It was around this time that I began a relationship with Non-cedo, a medical student from Medunsa, whom I knew from high-school days. She and I ended up having a son, Zukisa. Later, I also had a daughter, Azola, from a fleeting relationship with a BCom student named Dimi.

I was a poster child for irresponsibility and my actions almost derailed the studies of two talented people. It pains me when I cast my mind back to this period of my life.

I wasn't sorry when I was transferred from Pretoria to Afrox's gas operation centre in Germiston. I hooked up with an old school friend, Andile Mvinjelwa, also an engineer, who worked for Unilever in Boksburg. We shared a house in Vosloorus, which, although more of a melting pot than Atteridgeville, came with problems of its own.

The Katorus townships (Katlehong, Tokoza and Vosloorus) were being torn apart by civil war between Inkatha Freedom Party (IFP) aligned hostels – crammed with migrant workers from Natal – and the ANC's self-defence units, living in houses surrounding the hostels. Between the two was no-man's land.

There was no accounting for who would meet their end on any given day. If taxi drivers picked up the 'wrong' customers they'd be targeted – sometimes the passengers were ordered out, divided into ANC and IFP supporters, according to the language they spoke, and the isiXhosa speakers were executed. No one dared walk past a hostel or enter a no-go zone in case they were shot, or set alight.

Train stations were hotspots too and people were thrown off carriages and onto the tracks between Katlehong and Germiston. By that time I had a company car, a Nissan Skyline, so I could at least avoid public transport, but had to be careful where I drove in Vosloorus. I was wary of conversing with strangers and became a master of mixing up my lingo in case my words and phrases gave away my origins. Nobody knew on whose side police and security forces were, so it made life extremely difficult.

The most positive thing about this period was that I met my future wife. A friend, Mpumi Tyikwe, had invited both of us to his girlfriend Linda's birthday party. As I walked into the room my eyes settled on this beautiful lady talking to Linda. It was love at first sight.

Zoleka Ngalwa was in her final year of law at Unitra, so our early courtship involved much travelling between what was then the Transvaal and Transkei. When she finished her degree she came to live with me in Vosloorus, but eventually the violent environment got too much for us and we moved to Clarendon Court, across the road from the Brenthurst Clinic in Hillbrow. It was noisier than Vosloorus but there were fewer gunshots and we enjoyed the freedom of being able to walk the streets at any time. There were cinemas, music shops, bookshops, and restaurants and cafés that stayed open until all hours.

Zoleka was working for the ANC's legal department at what was then Shell House. The liberation movement was preparing to govern, with the help of countries such as Sweden and Denmark and without much assistance from the US and UK. Margaret Thatcher, British prime minister until late 1990, had met Nelson Mandela a few months after his release. She apparently told her foreign policy advisor Charles Powell that Mandela 'wasn't as intelligent as Robert Mugabe', but a great deal nicer. He was, she thought, an old-fashioned socialist with his head stuck in the 1950s. In a bid to make amends, and because he no doubt realised its strategic importance, her successor John Major offered to train ANC cadres in public administration. Zoleka was one of those chosen to attend a ten-week training course in the UK.

While she was away, our hearts grew fonder and I proposed to her, rather unromantically, over the phone.

On the day before I was meant to fetch Zoleka from the airport, I had a function at Afrox head office in Selby, after which I gave some colleagues a lift to a taxi rank in the city. As I was dropping them off, two minibuses blocked my way. I opened my window to find out what the problem was and had hardly opened my mouth to ask when I was dragged out, beaten up and the company Nissan was stolen.

It was 1992; car hijackings were a new phenomenon. At first, Afrox seemed disbelieving. I wondered if they thought I was somehow involved, but they gave me the benefit of the doubt.

Zoleka was more sympathetic when I met her at the airport, or so it seemed – I could hardly see her through my swollen eyes. For months after that I got petrol slips from strange destinations in the Cape and Natal, but tracing tactics weren't advanced back then and the car was never found.

We began the *lobola* (bride price) process immediately Zoleka was back in the country. My father enthusiastically led the negotiating process. He organised two of his close friends to accompany him. I was a tad concerned that he might overdo things. I knew he could be boastful at times, which could result in us overextending ourselves financially. But our families got on well and after months of to-ing and fro-ing between Mthatha and Cape Town, where Zoleka's parents lived, the deal was done.

That was enough tradition for us. Against our parents' wishes, we had one wedding – a church ceremony at St Martin's-in-the-Veld in Rosebank and a reception that was a far cry from what our parents had in mind. But it was the happy occasion we wanted. Our Joburg friends were amazing and made sure that our out-of-town visitors felt welcome.

Around this time I was approached by the HR manager at Tiger Brands, then Tiger Oats, a man named Neville Goldin. We had been colleagues at Afrox. One of the group's subsidiaries, Tastic Rice Corporation, needed an engineering manager to help consolidate its plants across South Africa. They wanted to build a processing plant in Pietermaritzburg, near the Durban harbour where the raw product came in by ship from Asia. The plants in Joburg and Cape Town were to be shut down. Neville made it clear that once I'd familiarised myself with operations on the Highveld, I would have to move to Natal.

After seven years with Afrox, I felt I'd paid my dues and I took up the offer, entering a new world in which I became familiar with technology such as blowers, belts and chutes – used to separate different grades of rice, remove stones, husks and discoloured grains. These were the days before optical sensors identified impurities.

Zoleka and I had bought our first home north of Joburg in Jukskei Park, now part of built-up Fourways. In those days it was remotely situated – and not racially integrated. But we had a comfortable house with all the modcons and it was with reluctance that we had to rent it out and move to Pietermaritzburg in mid-1993.

It wasn't a happy period for me, or for Zoleka. We rented a house close to the university and got a loan of R100 000 from the Small Business Development Corporation so that Zoleka could set up a clothing business in downtown Maritzburg. She's stylish, with a flair for fashion, and we short-sightedly imagined there'd be a gap in the market for a women's clothing boutique. She sourced clothing from warehouses in Joburg and Cape Town, but although many appreciated the upmarket designs, few opened their wallets. We were living in sleepy hollow, where a shop named 'Classic' had spectator value only.

To cap it all, our Fourways tenants – let's call them Mr and Mrs Whyte – stopped paying the rent. Just like that. They didn't take our calls and simply ignored our letters of demand for the monthly amount of R1 500 times twelve that they owed us after a year. We had to drive to Joburg one weekend and physically evict them. The place was a pigsty – broken doors and windows, trashed carpets and a swimming pool that resembled a swamp.

After two years in Maritzburg, we were relieved when paper-and-packaging giant Nampak recruited me and we returned to Joburg, bankrupt and bruised but wiser.

Nampak had long dominated packaging manufacturing. However, since sanctions had been lifted following the 1994 elections, it found itself faced with competition as cheaper products – sometimes by as much as 30 per cent – flooded the market. I was among twenty new recruits to head office in Sandton who were tasked with figuring out how to make the company competitive enough to take on Asian manufacturers.

Our group included Oupa Magashula, Tau Morwe, Motsoanetsi Lefoka, Vince Raseroka, Justice Luthuli, Sipho Thomo and Papi Moletsane. These aspirant black graduates made up the 'world-class college', the brainchild of Neil Cumming, Nampak's group HR director. He put in place a programme to bring workers closer to decision making, a method used to great effect in Japan, where those at the coalface come up with ideas to streamline operations. Japanese manufacturing techniques as an area of influential practices and philosophies had emerged in the post-World War II era and reached their height in the 1980s. Distinguishing characteristics included an emphasis on designing processes to optimise efficiency and a strong commitment to quality. Perhaps the most widely recognised suite of Japanese manufacturing techniques is known as the Toyota Production System (TPS), the core of which is just-in-time (JIT) production, or so-called 'lean manufacturing'. The pioneers of these methods were Taiichi Ohno, a former Toyota executive, and Shigeo Shingo, an eminent engineer and consultant. In his 1989 book *The Study of the Toyota Production System: From an Industrial Engineering Perspective*, known as the 'green book', Shingo identified the basic features of TPS:

> It achieves cost reductions by eliminating waste, be it staff time, materials, or other resources.
>
> It reduces the likelihood of overproduction by maintaining low inventories (non-stock) and keeps labour costs down by using minimal manpower.
>
> It drastically reduces production cycle time with innovations like the Single-Minute Exchange of Die (SMED) system, which cuts downtime and enables small-lot production.
>
> It emphasises that product orders should guide production decisions and processes, a practice known as order-based production.

These practices contrasted with traditional Western manufacturing of the pre-1980s, which tended to emphasise mass production, making use of full capacity, and the economies of scale that were presumed to follow.

It was at Nampak that my belief in making optimal use of people's skills to get ahead in business took root. By applying the concepts of total productive maintenance and autonomous work groups, we were able to incorporate the knowledge and experience of workers by empowering them to fix machinery and do changeovers rather than sit around waiting for technicians and mechanics. We built up autonomous teams that could disassemble plants, do changeovers and find the best methods to reduce inefficiencies.

Nampak was a great training ground for mid-career executives and I found myself gaining a deeper and all-round understanding of business, moving further away from engineering.

My profile enhanced, I began writing thought leadership pieces on 'world-class manufacturing' and felt confident enough to share my knowledge in publications such as *Productivity* SA, where one of my articles appeared under the title 'Why are South African organisations not serious about world-class competitiveness?':

> In-depth understanding is lacking in most South African boardrooms. Instead our top teams seem to perpetuate the myth that the upper reaches of management are a land of mystery and intrigue. However, companies like Ingersoll Rand and Federal-Mogul stand as beacons in our move towards world-class status . . .

Bill Mallory, MD of Ingersoll, confirmed that his organisation was able to manufacture sump pumps for use in the mining industry at its Alrode, Alberton plant and land them in New York at 25 cents cheaper than it costs to make them at the Pennsylvania plant . . .

What we need to do is to mobilise and pull together the intellectual resources of all employees in the service of our companies. It is only by drawing on the combined brainpower of all our employees and harnessing the miracle and spirit of the South African transformation that our organisations can face up to global competition.

For *Business Day* I wrote:

Millions of ordinary, psychologically normal South Africans will soon be facing an abrupt collision with the future.

As South African companies strive to become effective global players and the government pursues policies for implementing lean administration, country people will be subjected to unintended consequences of the private and public sector actions.

Firstly, initiatives like rightsizing, downsizing, re-engineering, outsourcing and benchmarking will inevitably send thousands of people at all levels into the ranks of the unemployed. Most of these people will be white-collar employees . . .

It would be naïve to think there will be fewer retrenchments in the future. According to American management guru Alvin Toffler, for companies to survive they will have to reduce their staff by half, pay the remaining half twice as much and have three times more output.

This is already happening in the US and Japan.

The question is whether South African employees are equipped to deal with this new reality. I believe they will find it increasingly painful to keep up with the incessant demand for change that characterises our time.

For most people, the future will arrive too soon.

*

I had found my groove at Nampak and was enjoying my role as managing consultant with Divpac – diversified packaging – a division that produced tin packaging for a range of products: toothpaste, shoe polish, aerosol.

Then in 1996 another world-class manufacturer, SA Breweries, approached me via an executive search agent, Klaasen Lekgetho. Search agents identify people who are not actively looking for jobs and headhunt them for employers with key positions to fill. The techniques we'd learned at Nampak were attractive to other companies. I was open to gaining engineering experience and told Klaasen I was interested.

I'd hardly done so when, out of the blue, I was approached by the Big Blue itself – International Business Machines – via Mpho Letlape, IBM SA's director of human resources. She said they were looking for individuals with deep industry expertise – in my case, manufacturing. Would I be interested?

I wasn't – and told her so. I was still an engineer at heart and knew nothing about sales, let alone IT sales. She explained it wasn't sales people they were looking for. IBM, under new global CEO Lou Gerstner, needed innovative industry experts who could connect with customers and pass the information on to technical types.

I'd never heard of Gerstner and did some reading.

In 1990, IBM had its most profitable year ever. But by 1993, the computer industry had changed so much that IBM was on a watchlist for extinction. IBM shares that had sold for $43 in 1987 crashed. On 1 April 1993, the day Gerstner took over, IBM stocks stood at $13.

The company's core mainframe business had been disrupted by the advent of the personal computer and the client server, and it couldn't compete with smaller and more diverse companies such as Microsoft.

In their book entitled *Computer Wars: How the West Can Win in a Post-*IBM* World*, Charles Ferguson and Charles Morris said IBM had experienced 'a monumental management fiasco . . . taking refuge in old technology when markets for big computers were shrinking . . . IBM's decline is a major and disturbing event . . . a finished force in the industry.'

I still didn't see myself making the move from pulp and packaging at Nampak to computer client services. Working at SAB made more sense to me. Mpho persisted. She said Gerstner had declined the IBM job when it was first offered to him because he'd felt he didn't have the technical know-how to handle it. He'd been president of American Express and then occupied the top job at RJR Nabisco, a conglomerate that sold tobacco and food products.

He'd been persuaded by the executive search team sent to recruit him that IBM wasn't looking for a technologist but a broad-based leader and change agent who knew what customers needed.

His move to IBM was widely acknowledged as 'a startling appointment'.

Another of the reasons he took the job was because of what he described as his 'gluttony for world-class challenges'. I have the same greed, perhaps not on a global scale, but I get bored easily and once I feel that all the problems have been fixed I tend to get itchy feet.

Mpho also explained that the job had legs: locally the future was an IBM led by South Africans not Americans, and there was a need to identify people who could be trained to take over the company. I would be an ideal candidate, she said, with my deep understanding of the industry verticals such as mining, manufacturing, retail, financial services, transport and telecommunication – each of which has unique characteristics that determine competitiveness. At Nampak, I was a manufacturing consultant focusing on Japanese techniques like Total Quality Management. This is what attracted IBM to me. They wanted industry experts who would engage customers at business rather than technical level.

I went to meet the GM of IBM South Africa, Mike Kos. He explained that at the time there was no specific role for me but as the new global model emerged, they would create one. I would also, at some stage, be posted overseas to be developed for a future leadership role.

Between Mike and Mpho, I was convinced.

Next I had to win over Zoleka. My wife didn't really get why I wanted to leave a good job that I knew all about for one I knew nothing about. I emphasised the prospect of an international assignment. We both enjoy travelling.

We decided to take a leap of faith.

Nobody believes me when I tell them Mteto used to be a party animal. He and I were both recruited by Nampak in the same period in the early '90s when affirmative action was taking ground. Before that, the corporate world was white and there was no place for a young black accountant like me. But then companies like Unilever, SAB and Nampak went on a recruitment drive and aspiring black graduates were given an opportunity. I worked at SAB then joined Nampak, which had a great training college that everyone raved about. The trainers were forward thinking and taught us the Japanese way of Total Productive Maintenance. New recruits would go on two-week courses at the college.

There were about twenty of us on course at a time and we were taught by people such as Neil Cumming, Rex Tomlinson and Derek van der Riet about how to improve productivity by getting workers to understand all aspects of the job so there was no waiting around for technicians on the factory floor. You had to take full ownership of the plant, not the narrow view of before where shift changes interrupted flow.

In practice it would create huge tension because the maintenance guys were white and the new black recruits came in and didn't need them any more. But we were young idealistic trainees and didn't think of that then.

Many of our group went on to become successful, like my

friend Mteto. He certainly showed signs of it. He would challenge our trainers at any opportunity, stretching logic wherever he could. He was at the centre of all arguments in class, finished his work first and was ready to party the night away.

After college ended for the day, we'd do our group projects together, then hit the pub of whatever conference centre we were staying at. We'd stumble to bed in the early hours and be back at lectures, bleary-eyed at 9 am.

As I said, what we learned at training didn't always translate on the shop floor. We were taught all these advanced new methods, but we didn't become the future general managers. We couldn't put our experience into practice because management was so scared of the white staff. In the mid-'90s external factors crept in: China's mass manufacturing began invading the South African market and import tariffs came down, and Nampak just couldn't compete with all the choices. To avoid being retrenched, I ended up at human resources. It was a typical white management move – 'let the darkies sort each other out' – and fire themselves. I did HR for the print paper division and had to close ten plants. Imagine. My ideals of being a world-class manufacturer faded and I became a first-class culling machine.

Mteto moved on to IBM – one of the richest, biggest organisations in the world. He later on led Microsoft South Africa – my younger brother was working there so we kept in touch. When I became SARS commissioner Mteto and I talked about how to change the aggressive corporate culture of technology companies who didn't like paying taxes. They would take their intellectual property, put it in a zero tax regime country and expatriate all the profits. Mteto is an ethical person and always does the right thing – morally, or in terms of governance.

I was a bit surprised when he went to MTN and I think the whole sorry strike saga must've got to him. I've never really sat down and talked to him about it, but would like to know his side of the story. The impression is that he capitulated to the unions. And that MTN lost market share under him. Maybe that's the only chapter in this book I will read!

On the plus side, Mteto is a proper leader, with long-term vision. Unlike me, who is unable to plan far ahead. I like short-term targets and can't think of where I'll be in three years. He is patient and strategic and able to see a much broader picture of industry. He's got me out of a few scrapes and given me plenty of good advice. He has great faith in black business and supports it wherever he can because he wants this country to be a success. As do we all.

– Oupa Magashula is Executive Chairman of CZ Electronics

Chapter 4

Into the Big Blue

13 September 1996
Dear Mteto

I have great pleasure in offering you a position with IBM South Africa as Senior Client Relationship Representative for Manufacturing, effective 1 October 1996.

Your manager will be Malcolm Taylor.

Your work location will be at IBM, Sandton. Any transfer to another IBM location will be in terms of the Company's Moving and Living Policy.

Please return the completed forms to me as soon as possible.

Yours sincerely
IBM Human Resources

I arrived at 70 Rivonia Road, Sandton, well before 9 am on Tuesday, 1 October 1996. Mpho Letlape, my only point of reference, was attending the World Women's Conference in Beijing and my new manager Malcolm Taylor, whom I'd never met, was completing an assignment in Europe. The only other person I knew, because he had interviewed me, was Vito Bonafede, who was in charge of cross-industry solutions. I knew him as a rally co-driver who, with Serge Damseaux, had won seven South African national championships. While I am a Formula One fanatic and I consider Michael Schumacher the best driver of all time, locally, I follow rally driving. I had been pleasantly surprised to hear that Vito was going to be my new manager. But by the time I started my job at IBM, Vito had been moved. I was disappointed. I would, in time, become familiar with the in-house joke that IBM actually stood for 'I've Been Moved'.

I was directed to an open-plan area in the manufacturing industry solutions unit that was to be my workspace. Once again I seemed to be the dark horse in a stable of pale faces.

When I introduced myself to Louis Schlebusch, one of the execs, he looked astonished and asked if I was in the right place. Once I'd assured him I really was, he confirmed that Vito had been shifted to outsourcing services and that Malcolm Taylor hadn't yet arrived from the Paris office to replace him. Judging by his tone, it didn't sound like a promotion for Vito.

I clearly couldn't sit around for two weeks waiting for Malcolm to arrive, so I asked Louis if there was an account I could start working on in the meantime. He said they were almost at the end of their financial year and that most accounts had been allocated. But there was a dormant account that had given them 'problems' and had been assigned to one of the reps, Tony Currin. Tony, too, looked taken aback at the sight of me. He said they had no black account managers covering the private sector, most being deployed to the public sector to deal with government. I made a mental note never to land up there. I hate being categorised.

The rest of the staff members were focused on closing deals

with customers. I later found out that they worked on commission, which explained their commitment. I had superficial knowledge of IT from Nampak, but the discussions I overheard then – full of acronyms and tech speak – were unfamiliar territory.

Tony filled me in on the dormant account and offered to introduce me to the customer, paper manufacturer Sappi. I knew a bit about Sappi – it had supplied paper for our packaging at Nampak – but I knew nothing about its IT requirements. Or anyone's for that matter.

There was only one way to learn. Tony and I went to Sappi's offices in Braamfontein to meet the information technology manager, Danie Scheun. As a black man entering an Afrikaner environment, I made a mental note to tread carefully. But Danie didn't appear to care what colour I was; he just wanted someone responsive. His view was that IBM was charging a lot for doing very little.

Sappi, I gathered, had a bad history with IBM, which had pulled out of South Africa in 1986 as a result of US sanctions. IBM had sold its South African subsidiary to an employee trust named ISG (Information Services Group), which would supposedly fulfil existing contractual obligations. Clearly, this hadn't worked out as well as it should have; when IBM returned to South Africa in 1994 it was to a disgruntled bunch of customers who felt they'd been abandoned without support. I assumed that Tony hadn't handled Sappi with enough care since then, because it had withheld payment of R12 million.

During our meeting, I sensed that if Danie saw I was willing to listen and if I was able to provide long-term solutions, the Sappi account could be revived. He told me that Sappi was a continuous operation that ran 24/7 and had unique problems, such as phone lines that ran through sugar-cane plantations getting burnt, or being chewed by cane rats. If systems were down, business was down.

Back at the office, I studied the history of the original deal, sifting through old contracts to find out what services the company had been promised and what it had been getting. I noticed that the rate Sappi had been charged for software wasn't in line with its original contract. I connected with other departments within IBM and found a helpful administrative manager, Wendy Bloom. Traditionally, IBM admin and sales didn't communicate much, let alone collaborate on accounts. Wendy helped me work out a settlement plan for Sappi's outstanding R12 million. It took me five months, but it was a valuable learning exercise and served me well in understanding IBM processes.

When Sappi made a decision to use SAP software for its resource planning, I did a presentation on why it should choose IBM hardware (RS6000) and suggested we also take over its information technology department and put in place dedicated IBMers to ensure that there was never downtime.

Sappi's executive committee, led by CEO Eugene van As and CFO Mike Turner, agreed to outsource to IBM SA. Vito Bonafede's sideways move paid off and he got his first win in the IT outsourcing space. We needed the support of IBM headquarters to deliver on this strategic project, so John Shimkus from the US came out to lead it as project executive. The deal was worth more than R40 million and made me one of IBM's top sales people for 1997.

I also took over the account of Sappi's competitor, Mondi,

which fell under IBM's small and medium business unit – a different department. I persuaded Louis Schlebusch, who had become my manager, that we should look at Mondi differently as it had huge potential and didn't have to be categorised as small business.

It was around that time that IBM bought Lotus Corporation. I tried hard to convince Mondi to invest in Lotus Notes instead of Microsoft Exchange. This is one of the battles I can say I lost dismally.

However, my course was set as an IT salesman selling IBM hardware, software and services. From knowing nothing about computers, I began to understand them well and enjoyed the work. I also came to realise that selling is part of our lives. Those who are masters at it – be it selling ideas, products or services – can influence the future. Selling is an important leadership competence.

*

When Lou Gerstner took over IBM, it was running out of cash; a bloated organisation with a reputation for looking after its employees 'from the cradle to the grave'. It owned prime office blocks that it didn't even use – such as the tallest building in Atlanta – and rented an entire floor in Manhattan for a million dollars a year. It even had an art collection worth $30 million.

This all changed in the '90s. In the biggest staff layoff in the history of American business, 45 000 people were fired in 1992 and the following year, a few months into Gerstner's tenure, a further 35 000 employees were let go.

In a memo to staff, he said:

I want you to know that I do not believe that those who are leaving IBM are in any way less important, less qualified . . . Rather we ALL owe those who are leaving an enormous debt of gratitude . . . Over the next few months, I plan to visit as many of our operations and offices as I can. And whenever possible, I plan to meet with many of you to talk about how together we can strengthen the company.

A staff member sent an email back:

GIMME A BREAK. Do some real work. Cut the order cycle time. Get new products on the markets. Listen to the folks that are not our current customers but would be if we had products for them . . . Do things that will keep you from having to trash more and more people every 6 months.

IBM South Africa's exodus began a few months into my new job. First, Country General Manager Mike Kos, who had interviewed me and made me all sorts of promises, was given his marching orders and returned to Europe. Lou Gerstner sent an American, Sal Faso, to replace Mike. He immediately announced that 200 IBMers had to go. It was a brutal move in a subsidiary consisting of just a thousand-odd employees.

I wasn't confident of keeping my job. I assumed their plan would be 'last in, first out', which might mean me. I had a few restless nights, but my fears were allayed when Sal told me I was part of their turnaround strategy. The promises Mike had made me remained. IBM, I would discover, had an excellent system for managing top talent. It kept detailed records of development plans for all employees on an executive resources programme, which focused on individuals with the potential to become executives.

> 1 May 1997
> Dear Mteto
>
> Your management is convinced that you are one of those who can lead the process of shaping and creating a new IBM. Your attitude towards success in our business gives proof thereof.
>
> In order to demonstrate our esteem in your abilities and to encourage your support in making the change happen for IBM South Africa, I am delighted to inform you about your participation in the IBM South Africa Retention Bonus.
>
> You will be awarded an amount four times your monthly salary, which will be indexed to the current IBM SA share price and paid in July 1999 based on the development of the stock price between now and June 1999.
>
> Let's work together to make it happen.
> Regards
> Sal

I was relieved, but many were not and until he left a year later, Sal Faso was known as 'The Executioner'. But he'd had no choice.

In February 1998, *Personal Finance* reported:

IBM, the 'big blue' looked more like the 'big bruise' after reporting a larger-than-expected full-year loss of R43 million. The share was one of the JSE's most notable losers yesterday, plunging to R5,30. Consequently market watchers seem reluctant to attach the tag 'recovery stock' to IBM just yet. But major restructuring has taken place and those with the guts to get in early could reap some substantial rewards.

Another of Faso's unpopular tasks was to delist IBM from the JSE. Unhappy investors were paid out R12 per share. My retention bonus was amended and aligned with global stock markets. I received a letter from Gerstner himself.

Dear Colleague

Congratulations on your IBM stock options award. This grant is a strong statement that your management team views you as critical to our future success.

Clearly, stock options align your interests with those of our shareholders. They give you a financial stake in the success of our company. And they can be very valuable in building your personal equity. But I trust you also recognize that this grant is, in fact, an opportunity, not a guarantee. Its ultimate value depends on each one of us – with our efforts to make IBM a winner in the marketplace.

As I look at the market opportunities before us, I have never been more confident in IBM's prospects. But I'm even more excited by the passion and energy I see in more and more

IBMers. I look forward to your continued contribution and leadership.

Sincerely
L.V. Gerstner, Jr
Office of the Chairman and Chief Executive Officer

In 1998 I had been acknowledged as one of IBM's top performers and received a Global Golden Circle Award for contributing to the company's revenue and profit objectives. The ceremony was held in Tenerife, the largest of the Canary Islands, off the coast of Morocco.

In the sixteenth century, the Canaries had been an important and strategic stop for traders between Africa, Europe and the Americas. Four centuries later, IBM's top international sales people gathered, more for fun than for strategy. I even went snorkelling.

Zoleka, who was pregnant with our daughter Anda, came with me. In the five years we'd been married we'd done a lot of travelling. Every fortnight or so we'd pack our weekend bags and head off to explore South Africa – Mpumalanga, the Garden Route, the Western Cape. Longer holidays would find us in Europe, or the US, broadening our minds and realising what a tiny place we occupied in the world.

Receiving the award made me aware that working for a global giant such as IBM could open many doors on my career path.

In October 2000, Mark Harris, who'd replaced Malcom Taylor as cross industry solutions executive, became country general manager for South Africa. He succeeded American Dennis Hearon. It was the first time a South African had been appointed to the position. The move was in line with IBM's global practice of placing local execs in top positions in the various countries in which they operated.

The understanding was that I would one day take over from Mark. In 1998 he'd appointed me to my first management position – telecoms and media executive. It was a business unit that wasn't doing well and covered emerging companies such as MTN, Vodacom and MultiChoice, together with old firms like Telkom, SABC and Eskom. The sales people were a disparate group who didn't plan or operate as a team. Nor did they have much patience with the vagaries of parastatals. At first, it irritated my new team that I was always asking them who they'd seen and what deals they'd closed. Some felt that their relationships with their customers were being questioned, but most of them – Leon Botha, Lillian Barnard, Cecelia Jofre, Servaas Venter, Freddie Masinga, Yogesh Ranchod – understood that we needed a new approach to turn around a failing unit. They did an excellent job.

One team member – Joseph Makhabane, who was in charge of utilities – made no secret of the fact that he wasn't happy. Joe had been with IBM since April 1994 and took exception to my appointment. At first I thought it was because he was older and had been with the company longer than me, but I later gathered that wasn't the only issue. He didn't like the idea of working for a black person. So in my first leadership role, one of the people I'd assumed I could rely on for support resented me.

He resigned a few months later. I wasn't sorry, but I took it as a warning. I couldn't fail and allow the Joes of the world to say, 'I told you so.'

My unit began making inroads with some big players such as MultiChoice and Telkom, as well as Vodacom, which had started out in 1994 with 50 000 subscribers and increased that number tenfold. Its call centre agents couldn't handle the influx, so we set up a voicemail service – the country's first. Our WebSphere Voice Response served incoming customer care calls, as well as revenue-generators such as phone voting for shows such as *Big Brother* and *Idols*.

We tried to persuade the SABC to sign us up to digitise its archives so that news clips and footage could be available in an online library. But the executives of that era, Zwelakhe Sisulu and co., just didn't get it; they were unable to see beyond analogue.

Telkom, under new CEO Sizwe Nxasana, was amenable to modernisation. But historically, Telkom and IBM had a bad relationship because of the latter's withdrawal of support during sanctions. This changed when a 30 per cent stake in Telkom was sold to a consortium that included the US-based southwestern Bell Corporation (now AT&T). The new IT infrastructure executive was an American, Eugene Pinto, who understood the value of IBM products and reached out to us. He particularly liked our mainframe specialist, Joe Makhoba. He made Joe and me famous by buying the biggest S390 mainframe to digitally transform Telkom.

We updated Telkom's inferior technology, its IT billing system, and connected phone lines to digital exchanges for caller line ID and electronic answering.

We were acknowledged as a dynamic and successful team. That seemed to be Mark Harris's cue to move me to the next under-performing IBM business division. A friend, Anne Whitehead, who I'd got to know when I first started in the manufacturing division, wondered if I was being set up for failure. I wasn't sure, but decided to view it as a positive move.

The new unit to which I was assigned – small and medium enterprises – was going nowhere. Performance and sales figures were dismal. There was no effort to actively pursue new deals. IBM had always been a large company, very good at selling to large enterprises. It simply wasn't in its DNA to bother with smaller customers. So Mark had discussions with Louis Guelette, the vice president of SMB in Central Europe, Middle East and Africa (CEMA) and they decided to bring me in to find innovative ways to establish deeper relationships with SMBs in South Africa – potentially a huge market.

The first thing I had to do was get rid of dead wood – politely called 'management-initiated separation'. There were 50 people in the unit and fifteen of them had to get the chop – mostly managers, which wasn't easy. I worked closely with HR and tried to make it as painless as possible. But there are invariably tears and tantrums in a process like this.

Next I needed to work out a strategy. How do you cover so many SMB customers with so few resources? It couldn't be done internally, so we decided the most effective approach would be to forge relationships with IT resellers, then offer them incentives to sell IBM products.

Our telesales teams would get a lead or cold call companies, identify their needs – be it storage, software or upgrades – then pass them on to IT resellers to close the deal. To promote our products, we invited customers to attend joint marketing activities with our new partners. These IT resellers became key to our strategy and we shed our perceived 'big boy' status and built up our client base – despite not having enough resources, or reach. I was constantly on the hunt for collaborations and structured partner programmes, as well as trying to beat revenue targets.

The end of the financial year at IBM is 31 December and we would spend our Christmas holidays chasing deals to make those targets, even if it meant visiting business owners at their beach homes. We worked on a commission basis, so there wasn't too much complaining from staff.

In time, our double-digit revenue growth began attracting the attention of the top brass in Europe. SMB was new territory for IBM – nobody had a clear formula, but the South African model of assigning people to IT resellers to get them deals and discounts seemed to be a winner.

Andy Williams, the vice president for the Europe, Middle East and Africa SMB sector, came out from Paris. What was IBM South Africa doing right? How could the rest of the region emulate SA's approach? He was asking the right questions. The role of head office is to identify and roll out best practices. And my unit had made itself relevant by differentiating itself from competitors; collaborating and forming structured win-win partnerships with smaller players. And treating them with respect – the way my mother treated her customers back in Tabase.

I joined IBM South Africa human resources in July 1995, and one of my tasks was to drive transformation. At the time we had many expatriate managers who needed to be replaced by locals when their assignments ended. Finding these locals was easier said than done, so I found help from executive search agents.

One of the headhunters we worked with to fill existing and emerging vacancies was Klaasen Lekgetho.

One day I got a call from him saying I had to meet this young man who was leaving Nampak to join South African Breweries. He was an engineer with an MBA. Klaasen thought that Mteto would fit IBM better than SAB.

When we met I was bowled over by his humility and depth, but most importantly I saw talent that would simply thrive at IBM. I had been with IBM for fifteen years by then and I knew how the organisation developed, nurtured, and invested in talented people. I was determined to convince Mteto to decline the SAB offer, after he had accepted it, and join IBM.

The value proposition to him was that IBM was an industry that lacked African people; it was dynamic and interesting, and definitely more challenging and exciting than making, bottling and selling beer. IBM's different sectors, products and services were great toys to play with. There was opportunity for innovation and for changing lives. Beer, as I told him, is just beer.

Mteto was very conscious of knowing nothing about IT, and as a principled person felt he had an obligation to SAB. Klaasen and I worked on him and in the end an apology was sent to SAB and a new era began.

Mteto was interviewed by the country general manager, Mike Kos, and I made a case for a three-month 'get to know IBM' induction programme to get him to understand the IT industry before deciding where to place him.

In my heart and in my mind though, I thought that the Small and Medium Business division, SMB, would be the best fit for him, given his experience at Afrox, Tiger Brands and Nampak.

Mteto started his extensive induction into IBM and the IT industry and in no time became a highly valued member of the team and made a mark in the SMB division, which he went on to head a mere three years later.

Mteto is the only person that I know of in IBM who got promoted whilst on assignment at EMEA headquarters in Paris. I had left IBM by that time, but his reputation and news of his success filtered back.

Mteto and I remain in contact, and consciously work on getting together for an hour every twelve weeks or so.

– Mpho Letlape is founder and chairman of
Lethushane Properties

I had the privilege of working for Mteto in 1998 as IBM sales representative for the telecommunications industry solutions unit. It was clear from the onset that he was destined for greatness. I came to know him as a quiet, thoughtful leader who did more in deeds than in words, but I also saw him grow into a leader able to assert himself in such a powerful way that many would listen. Working for him was very brief yet impactful; he had the ability to make you want to strive for so much more. We once again crossed paths when we were both assigned to Paris, France. He went ahead of me and when I got there became my sounding board for many things. I vividly remember soliciting his input about my rental apartment location and other trivial matters, which he was always willing to assist with. We were located on the 37th floor of the big Paris IBM HQ Building and I would now and then pop into his office to ask for advice on something that challenged me.

Mteto returned home in 2005 and I ended up staying in Europe until the end of 2009. Although we didn't remain in contact during this period, we re-established our relationship upon my return, with little effort.

I left IBM after fifteen years in 2011 to start my own business and, as I drove out of the gate on my final day, I called Mteto to boldly ask him for his support and advice on my journey into the unknown. In the three years that I ran my business, he was never too busy to pick up or return my phone calls and my meeting requests were honoured time and time again. His leadership style is clothed in dignity, humility and humanity. I have consulted him about all my career moves and I am grateful to have the time and attention of a person whose career journey has been intentional, inspirational and impactful.

– Lillian Barnard is MD of Microsoft SA

Chapter 5

The Global Circle

The road to success has many tempting parking places.
– Steve Potter

I shouted out and began running, then cursed as the bus whizzed past me. The driver didn't even slow down. I'd been strolling, thinking it would at least wait twenty seconds for me to get on. I'd familiarised myself with bus routes and train timetables and knew that it took 45 minutes to get to IBM HQ in La Défense in the Paris CBD. Now I would be late. For a brief moment I found myself longing for an Mzansi minibus taxi, which would have ramped the pavement to pick me up and got me to the train station at breakneck speed. It was a stark reminder that things in this part of the world happen on time and without much humanity.

On the train my fellow passengers were introspective – immersed in their devices or newspapers – without ever making conversation. I would become one of them, travelling with the same people every day for four years, yet never acknowledging them. In hindsight, I wish I had. I think they wanted to engage; it just wasn't in their nature.

My boss in the Paris office was the same person I'd reported to from Joburg. Louis Guelette, a Belgian, was now vice president SMB sales. During the week he lived in Paris; on Fridays he would go home to Belgium for the weekend, an hour and twenty minutes by train.

I was glad my long-distance commuting days were over. For the first two months I'd done the same. Every Thursday night I had flown out of Charles de Gaulle Airport, gone straight to IBM's Rivonia office on my arrival, spent Friday night and Saturday at home with Zoleka and Anda, and flown back to Paris on Sunday night, in time for work the next morning. It was quite a lifestyle, but there was no other way to do it until my work permit had been sorted, our house sold and our belongings packed and shipped.

We hadn't wanted to move to Europe. I'd had my eye on a transfer to the US. On a training trip in New York, I'd gone to IBM's HQ in Armonk to chat to Marc Lautenbach, the global head of small business, about an international posting. I liked him enormously and he suggested that I take up a position as his executive assistant. But I needed to wait another eight months until a vacancy came up. The idea appealed to me; it would mean exposure to all the right people within IBM. But I didn't want to wait.

Back in Joburg I had discussions with Country General Manager Mark Harris about finding an international posting and getting someone to take over my job as SMB executive in South Africa. The latter was solved sooner than we thought when Stewart van Graan, who had been executive of IBM's personal computers division, returned home after a stint in the US. But it left me jobless. Mark told me that in the meantime I should sort out the public sector division. As I've said, I enjoy challenges such as infiltrating the ivory towers of traditional South African business, but dealing with government felt to me as if I was being typecast: black person deals with black government. I didn't want to get stuck there. I wanted something completely different.

IBM has four operating geographies – North America, South America, Europe Middle East and Africa (EMEA) and Asia Pacific (AP). The EMEA headquarters was in Paris and among its operating regions was Central Europe, Middle East and Africa (CEMA), which had a German general manager, Johann Weihen. On one of his trips to South Africa, he'd casually said that if I ever needed anything, I should contact him. So I sidestepped Mark and did just that.

Within two days he'd spoken to Andy Williams (EMEA Vice President SMB) and found a position for me. 'Come to Paris and build up our SMB channels.'

Mark's problem of where to place me was solved.

Lou Gerstner once called EMEA the 'mightiest of all nobles' – 90 000 employees operating in 44 countries with duplicate infrastructure and independent systems. Revenue had peaked at $27 billion in 1990 and had since declined. To correct this, he said, power had to be shifted from these 'geographical fiefdoms' towards central management.

There was resistance. Regional heads wanted to maintain their autonomy. On a visit to Europe, Gerstner discovered that employees weren't receiving his group emails because the head of Europe was intercepting them, saying they were 'inappropriate and hard to translate'. Gerstner summoned the man to Armonk and told him that all employees belonged to IBM and if he couldn't shape up to the new global structure, he should ship out. He did, a few months later.

By the time I got to France in 2001, IBM had consolidated its worldwide marketing and sales, breaking the customer base into industry groups – areas such as banking, government, insurance – and a category covering small- and medium-size businesses. And that was where I fitted in. South Africa's SMB successes were to be emulated in Europe.

According to IBM research, the opportunity growth rate of the SMB marketplace, at an average of thirteen per cent, exceeded that of large enterprises. But it needed 'solutions' – an integrated bundle of hardware, software, services and finance to access information and capabilities that larger organisations already had.

On my first day, I sat in Louis Guelette's office in Tour Descartes, also known as IBM Tower, an impressive parallelepiped structure that looks out onto an array of glass-and-steel high-rise buildings. He said: 'You are here and there is no one like you. I don't know how you are going to be received, but what you should know is that I have confidence in you. I know your capabilities. Let's walk this journey together.'

I felt encouraged and empowered by his honesty and support, but actually found no problem adapting. Granted, I was different; the only black African professional in the office, but my colleagues came from all over the world and embraced diversity. And the Mandela phenomenon was still strong. I told everyone we were born in the same district back home and spoke the same indigenous language, which seemed to impress.

I stayed in a hotel in La Défense, close to work. But I knew that when Zoleka and Anda joined me, living in that area would not be an option. Apartments were out of our price range and anything vaguely affordable near the city would be so tiny that our three-year-old would have no space to be a child. My wife and daughter came over for what IBM calls a 'look-see' trip and we searched outlying suburbs, eventually finding a house in Feucherolles, about 30 km west of the city centre. The house belonged to a family that was being transferred to Spain to work for General Electric. The monthly rental was €1 750 – expensive – but a whole lot cheaper than Paris itself. It had a garden and even a garage for a car. In the centre of Paris, garages are more expensive than entire houses in South Africa. We signed the lease and Zoleka returned home to pack up our lives for the start of a defining chapter.

I had said my goodbyes. My siblings had given us a farewell at my youngest brother Langa's place in Midrand. All our friends were there to wish us well. We were entering the unknown. We'd always imagined living and working in America, but never in Europe.

I had felt particularly sad leaving my parents. They had never understood Zoleka and me spending so much time travelling when we were in our late twenties, instead of settling down and providing them with a host of grandchildren. Now, no sooner had we had a child than we were off again – and not just for a short holiday. My mother had undergone a knee operation and her health had deteriorated. She'd given up the shop and had lost her spark. As I gave her a last hug, I felt as if I probably wouldn't see her again. She said, as she often did when we parted:

'Mteto mntanam – umphathe kakuhle umolokazana wam. Ndi-yamthanda umaThole.' (My child, look after my daughter-in-law. I love her dearly.)

*

Zoleka and Anda arrived to join me in August 2001, summer, and we moved into our new home. Feucherolles was green and pretty and wooded. We bought a second-hand car, a Ford Focus, and got to know the neighbourhood. The outer suburbs of western Paris are home to a large English-speaking expat community, so we could at least converse with our neighbours in a language we understood. Zoleka began looking around for a crèche for Anda and learning the difference between a *boulangerie* and a *patisserie*.

With Louis Guelette as my mentor, and with colleagues who spoke English and who seemed genuinely interested in me, I slowly settled in to a Parisian lifestyle.

It wasn't as easy for Zoleka: she didn't know a soul. At times I felt bad for having brought her to this unfamiliar world. Most of the time she coped, but when winter set in she became frustrated. She hated the cold, the radiators didn't work properly and she couldn't get them fixed because it was so hard to communicate her request. Shopping was an ordeal and finding her way around on her own took courage. It was painful for me to see her like that and I would rush home from work in the evenings to be her sounding board. It became obvious to both of us that she would have to learn the language. I made inquiries at work and they organised French lessons.

In six months her life changed. By becoming fluent in French, she became the family leader, ordering our food at restaurants, asking for directions, speaking to trades people and making friends with parents at Anda's Montessori school.

From a growth perspective, the Paris posting was a good one for me. My first big challenge came three months after my arrival: I had to share my strategy with SMB executives in the EMEA region. The truth was I wasn't ready. But instead of saying so, or asking for assistance, I agreed to give a PowerPoint presentation at a conference chaired by the boss, Andy Williams, and attended by the entire region. Even Stewart van Graan, who had replaced me in Joburg, was there. Expectations were high, my performance low. I knew the subject, but somehow couldn't articulate my ideas coherently. Delegates didn't hold back when it came to criticism and told me afterwards that my strategy was unclear, my content muddled and that I had given them no clear direction. It would have been so easy for me to have run my presentation by Louis in the days before I gave it – but I hadn't wanted to subject myself to negative feedback. So I'd blundered on. I felt that I'd blown it and feared being sent back home. Andy, in his polite British way, didn't say a word. Fortunately my track record still held weight with him.

But in early 2002, Andy was replaced by Massimo Bonciano, a chain-smoking Italian who had done an amazing job of building IBM's software division in a company known for its hardware.

I'd heard he wasn't the nicest of characters and that he had a ruthless streak, with little patience for non-achievers. My heart dropped when he called me in and asked what was going wrong. He must've heard I was messing up. I told him what I'd done with SMBs in South Africa – identifying new categories of customers and introducing incentives for small business partners based on sales targets – but that I didn't know how to make this strategy work in my new environment. He listened and said little.

I had sleepless nights. I'd heard there was restructuring and that decisions were being made about who to keep and who not. I was so terrified of being axed by Mr Fix-it Bonciano that I didn't even tell Zoleka. Imagine, with her and Anda finally settled, having to return to South Africa with my tail between my legs?

Instead, to my utter amazement, I got a promotion. I was to report directly to Massimo, on the same level as my old boss Louis. I was now director for SMB channels. I was elated and relieved, but a little uncomfortable that some of those who'd reported to Louis now reported to me. But he was gracious and pleased for me and continued to guide me in what became a hugely pressurised job. The turnaround of IBM's relationship with SMBs in Europe would be directly related to whatever steps my team and I put in place.

It was satisfying to be promoted to this level in a country where there was no affirmative action, nor any assumptions about my capabilities. A business in trouble was looking for the best person.

I recall receiving a note from a colleague in South Africa – Keith Johnson – wanting to know if I was coping in Europe. He was concerned for me. It was such a pleasure sending him the formal promotion announcement. Timing is everything, I thought.

I developed a strong relationship with Massimo, who was tough and demanding, with little respect for other peoples' views

102

on what he saw as trivial issues, such as blowing smoke all over everybody in meetings. He was interested only in delivery. I had to fill him in on every move as I forged partnerships with businesses in Europe. Communication was something he valued above all else: it was his way of getting things right through other people. I worked closely with another Italian, Giuseppe Guliani, who also had an engineering background. I hear that nowadays he plots the best performance of sailing boats in competitive racing. But then our days at IBM were spent re-structuring our business model so that potential partners saw the value of focusing on SMBs. There were 19 million compa-nies in EMEA, most of them looking for solutions, but too small to have an IT section to see to their needs. We offered them end-to-end solutions through business partners they trusted, introducing express versions of IBM products that were easy to install and operate, and were appropriately priced.

As Massimo told Ireland's online publication *Silicon Republic*: 'You have to have an ecosystem around them made up of sys-tem integrators, local software vendors, resellers, value-added resellers, consultancy groups – and the real challenge is to how to put all these players together and to be able to deliver to the customer what they are looking for.'

It was quite a life. For the first time ever, through Massimo, I had access to a private jet – IBM EMEA had two on permanent standby – and we would regularly fly to European and Middle Eastern cities, building sales teams to influence buyers for our hardware and software. We would sometimes find ourselves in Stuttgart in the morning, Milan in the afternoon and back in Paris in the evening. I made a conscious effort not to take this high life for granted. As someone once said: 'When you're accustomed to privilege, equality feels like oppression.'

You can get too used to things that don't belong to you.

*

By that time, Anda was attending the British School of Paris, founded in the 1950s to provide an English education to expats in France. Like me, she'd started her learning early. One night in late May 2003, when she was five, she came into our room. She said she'd seen my mother, her grandmother, and that she'd spoken to her. We assumed she'd been awoken by a dream and didn't really understand what she was talking about.

The next day we got the message that my mother had died.

In Xhosa tradition, the ancestors act as intermediaries between the living and the dead and visit the living in dreams. I don't doubt that my mother came to Anda to tell her that she was moving on to the spiritual world. It helped me deal with her death. It's a huge regret for me that I wasn't there at the end.

On the flight home from Paris via Joburg to Mthatha, I reflected on my mother's life. She'd taught me valuable lessons, mainly about how to treat people. At her funeral it was evident how many lives she had touched. I delivered the eulogy and spoke about her sacrifices in making sure her children were educated. Not only us: she'd put other people's children through school too and had supported women whose husbands were away in exile. She'd done what she had to do and done it well. The funeral was a reunion, with all of us – my half-brothers and -sisters included – focused on giving the matriarch the send-off she deserved. In her passing, my mother united her extended family.

My father was bereft. Although he'd watched her health declining, he hadn't mentally prepared himself for life without his partner of more than 40 years. After her death, he lost his sense of purpose, as well as his eyesight, and didn't last for many years.

I still feel them with me at times – the parents my soul chose – and I like to believe that they continue to nudge me in the right direction.

– Bhele, why don't you do medicine?

– You do what you want, Dlambulo . . .

I remember buying popcorn from a stand near the Eiffel Tower and riding a carousel nearby. I remember doing cartwheels in the kitchen and injuring my toe. I remember attempting to write a story on my father's laptop but giving up when I realised I could not spell 'once'. I remember pretending to sleep walk so I could watch television with my mother after bedtime. I remember the cherry tree in our garden and my neighbour with whom I played regularly, despite our inability to communicate. I remember our long driveway and how it would be coated in a thick layer of snow during the winter. In essence, my memories of France follow more of a montage format than distinct, continuous sequences of memories.

Nor do I have vivid memories of my grandparents, particularly of my grandmother, as she passed away when I was very young. When I was five, I dreamt that I had attended my grandmother's funeral. The following day, she passed away. This led me to believe that I have a strong spiritual connection with both of my grandparents – one that transcends physicality. My grandfather's smile is engrained in my memory; it was warm and genuine. His blindness did not hinder his smile. My last memory of him was viewing him in his casket – smiling even then. I do not know whether or not this is a confabulation. Regardless, it's the snapshot I preserve in my mind.

The most important aspect of my grandfather and my father's

upbringing, which he has passed on to me, is the value of education. Education changed the trajectory of my father's life and thus my life. His ambition and drive, coupled with his mother's encouragement, allowed him to uplift himself, his family and his community. He has afforded me the opportunity to dream and achieve big, with no limitations, while setting up a future full of opportunity for the succeeding generations of this family.

Fundamentally, our brains function similarly – practical, logical, calculated. However, outside of academics, my way of thinking tends to be more emotional and abstract. I would say we both have a way with words, but our medium of communication differs. My father is able to articulate his thoughts verbally clearly and succinctly with no preparation. I can do the same through the written word. If you ask me to give an impromptu speech, or ask him to write a creative piece, we would both struggle.

Not many things visibly anger my father. However, someone abandoning the values that govern his life – integrity, honesty and respect – can anger him. Additionally, anyone who jeopardises their ability to fulfil their potential upsets my father. Whether it be a lack of effort or not taking advantage of an opportunity, anything that hinders someone's progress and ultimate success is disappointing for him, especially if he cares for you.

The only time I see him out of his depth is when he is attempting to put together an outfit for an event. Typically, it will require my mother pulling out numerous suits, shirts and ties and my father modelling them until they reach a mutual agreement. And he tends to over-react when he is ill. For example, when he had a persistent sore throat once he took himself to the Emergency Room to seek immediate medical attention.

My father has this child-like essence that manifests in his laugh and his playfulness. Now that I am away at university in the US, I miss his 'unique' dance moves; I miss the way he walks in from work and says, 'Hello, beautiful ladies'; I miss him falling asleep around 8 pm on the couch. He has the type of personality that lifts your spirits and brings you comfort and security. I miss his contribution to the atmosphere of my home. Two people who never fail to make my father laugh are my mother and Trevor Noah.

I have always admired my parents' relationship. They communicate effectively, trust each other, love each other wholly, have an equal power balance and maintain a sense of fun through banter and humour. I believe that these qualities constitute a life-long partnership. I strive to find a partner with whom I can share these qualities.

– Anda Nyati is a pre-medical neuroscience
undergraduate student at Johns Hopkins University, Baltimore

Mteto Nyati was introduced to me when I was the IBM VP in charge of the largest part of IBM Business (commercial market, business partners, marketing, next-generation business) for the EMEA emerging markets.

I got to know a rather shy young man with a ready smile and a willingness to contribute. He had an ability to work out solutions to problems and was hands-on when it came to teamwork. We decided to make him responsible for the revenue target of the SMB sector in South Africa, an area with limited resources that needed cooperation with business partners – a complex world that he did not know very well. Complex because such relationships can be with both partners and competitors and very much depend on the right deal being struck.

Such management requires maturity and diplomacy and I was surprised to find these qualities and characteristics in a young man with little practical experience of the business.

Mteto kept developing himself and executive management agreed that it would be in the best interests of IBM South Africa, where we wanted him to return, if he was given an international assignment at IBM EMEA HQ, by then in Paris. Mteto accepted the challenge and moved to Paris with his family.

Paris was a different kind of job, requiring the ability to co-ordinate business activities across Europe, the Middle East and Africa. Here Mteto demonstrated another quality – an ability to successfully adapt himself to a completely new human environment, away from everything that was familiar on the home front.

We had discovered a potential leader, a bright man with a high level of attention for others and an incredible ability to motivate people around him – not only those who reported to him, but also his peers.

There are people able to unite teams wherever they are – Mteto is one of them.

I enjoyed working with this great man.

– Louis Guelette is the president of BOPartner France and on the advisory board of the Midis Group

Chapter 6

Yale World Fellow

They are trailblazers: disruptive thinkers and bold, original voices in their fields. They are practitioners from all sectors, poised for the next step . . . They can't help themselves: wherever they go, they profoundly shape their surroundings for the better. They are entrepreneurs, activists, journalists, artists, and politicians. They are doctors, lawyers, soldiers, artists and business executives. They are the World Fellows.

– Yale World Fellows website

I arrived at Yale University in the autumn of 2004, Zoleka and Anda in tow. Fortunately, like me, the two of them are always ready for another adventure. This time it was to be in New Haven, Connecticut, a coastal city north-east of New York, above Long Island. It's a very liberal, well-organised place with great education, and Yale is its biggest taxpayer and employer. We enrolled Anda at Wintergreen School, not far from the campus. Owing to her expat education in Paris she sounded like a little Brit, but we had no doubt that she would fit in at her new school.

As my spouse, Zoleka was allowed to study whatever she liked, so she continued her French, while I became part of a structured programme of daily lectures and debates. We lived on the campus, immersed in academia.

I was about to turn 40 and I couldn't think of a better way to take stock of my life and assess where I was at. The long-term plan was still that I should head IBM South Africa, but my old mentor, Marc Lautenbach, had thought a stint at Yale would serve me well, so he'd nominated me to the Yale World Fellows Program. I was one of about two thousand people nominated globally and eighteen of us were chosen from countries other than the US, which wasn't eligible. It's Yale's contribution to globalism and a way of building connections with the rest of the world through potential future leaders. The year before me, Raenette Taljaard – our youngest ever MP – had been selected from South Africa, the year after me, 2005, it was Nicky Newton-King, CEO of the Johannesburg Stock Exchange (JSE).

In 2004 there were just two of us from business, a fellow named Nachiket Mor, who was director of one of India's largest development banks, and me. The rest were an eclectic bunch – a congressman from the Philippines who specialised in clean air; a Russian corporate governance reformer; the advisor to the prime minister of Kosovo; the publisher of Morocco's first independent business newspaper; the director of an Israeli legal advocacy group for Arab rights; a programme development manager from Malawi named Paul Kwengwere; Northern Ireland's top government official in youth development; and one of China's most influential investigative journalists, Michael Ma (Ma Jun), who had written a book entitled *China's Water Crisis*.

I had taken a sabbatical from my post as director of SMB channels for IBM Europe, Middle East and Africa but continued receiving my salary, as well as a stipend from Yale. Not a bad way to spend six months.

The *Yale Bulletin & Calendar* wrote:

Reflecting on why he chose to take part in the Yale World Fellows Program, South African IBM executive and 2004 World Fellow Mteto Nyati said: 'I decided to invest this time to take a step back from all the things I am involved in, develop new strategies and close knowledge gaps . . . a very worthwhile investment. I have never been on any program that offers what this program does.

We were exposed to classical philosophical texts and current academic research and even had individual coaching in public speaking. We had a variety of guest lecturers, seminars on issues such as Aids, energy and terrorism and how they affected our countries – topics that, although hugely relevant, I might not normally encounter in the workplace. The Fellows from Myanmar, Georgia and Russia said that in their countries, Aids simply wasn't a topic of discussion; their governments acted as if it didn't exist. Nachiket commented that this was probably because politicians didn't benefit from prevention; their only concern was how to win the next election. An Iranian fellow, Emran Razaghi, from that country's health ministry, said that in Iran prevention programmes were largely ineffectual and that nobody cared. I disagreed, telling them that in my country, voters followed the numbers to gauge the value of prevention programmes and that politicians were judged on that. In August 2003, the South African cabinet had approved a plan for universal antiretroviral (ARV) treatment, thanks to active citizenry.

My days were full and busy: we went on trips to New York and Washington and wrote papers for university publications.

I wrote about our labour laws and the effect they had on our youth:

<blockquote>

South Africa's educated youth carries the full burden of our restrictive labour laws. What started as a quest for fair labour practices ended up as protection against new entrants. SA's labour laws protect the status quo. They stifle change where change is demanded. The laws protect employee rights well, but in a post-apartheid era, where economic growth and job creation are the main goals, they have become a drag.

</blockquote>

In another paper entitled 'SA Needs to Root its Growth in Vital Values', I wrote:

<blockquote>

South Africa's racist past left its people scarred. SA has to instil empowering values in its society to heal these apartheid scars. Values such as candour, entrepreneurship and partnership need to underpin SA's transformation agenda. They can forge a bridge between SA's past and its future. These values will also communicate to society what must be cherished . . . Values are to a national agenda what soul is to a human being.

</blockquote>

My writing improved and I gained confidence in my ideas and beliefs. I was surprised when then President Thabo Mbeki quoted from an article I'd written while at Yale. While delivering the annual Nelson Mandela Lecture in November 2004, Archbishop Tutu had criticised the Mbeki government's policies on poverty, Aids, Zimbabwe and the enrichment of the black elite. Mbeki had hit back, accusing Tutu of 'indecently resorting to empty rhetoric'. The spat continued into 2005; in the *ANC Journal*, Mbeki wrote a piece entitled 'Who shall set the national agenda?':

> Mteto Nyati, in an article that appeared in *Business Day* on 7 December 2004 . . . commented on the Tutu-Mbeki controversy. Nyati said: 'In South Africa the fight is really about who sets the national agenda. Should it be the African National Congress (ANC) or should it be the white elite? On the one hand the black majority government believes that it has a mandate to set the country's priorities. On the other hand the white elite believes its role is to provide thought leadership to the black majority. However, this group's real interest is to protect its wealth and lifestyle. This tension manifests itself in many ways . . .'

As Mteto Nyati has said, our current reality is that, to protect its interests, our own contemporary 'white elite' continues to believe that it has a responsibility to provide 'thought leadership' to an African population that is 'intellectually at zero', coming from nowhere and carrying nothing with it, especially in the context of the late twentieth and early twenty-first centuries.

At this point, we should explain that we take it that when he referred to 'the white elite', Nyati was not talking about the overwhelming majority of our white compatriots. Rather, he was talking about a small minority that believes that it knows best what is good for our country.

Accordingly, we will refer to this group, which includes both black and white South Africans, as 'the elite', without Mteto

Nyati's racial qualification. Obviously this group does not hold the same views on all questions. However, what brings it together is a shared political and ideological platform that is at variance with the ANC's own platform . . . as Nyati said, 'The black majority government believes that it has a mandate to set the country's priorities.' On the other hand, the 'elite' enjoys the strategic advantage that it has better daily possibilities to communicate its views to the general public . . .

Even the 'elite' of which Mteto Nyati spoke tries its best to secure its popular legitimacy by presenting itself as being, indeed, the most loyal tribune of the aspirations of the people as a whole. Conversely, it works hard to project its principal opponent, the ANC, as the principal enemy of those aspirations . . .

My participation in public discourse back home made me feel less like returning to France. When I heard that Alan Coward, the general manager of IBM Global Services in South Africa was resigning, I got hold of Massimo Bonciano and said I wanted the position. It would effectively make me second in charge of the company in South Africa, after Mark Harris. I knew if I didn't get the job, my route to the top might be impeded. Massimo contacted Andrew Creasey, the UK-based vice president of global services, and I flew from New York to London to be interviewed by him. I was delighted when I was appointed, although Mark thought I should've taken another international posting, in China or India. But the stint at Yale with a bunch of people actively working for change in their countries had made me aware of how much I missed mine. At the end of the Yale World Fellows Program we went back to Paris, packed up and headed home.

IBM South Africa's IT services business wasn't in good shape. The IBM Global Services team hadn't done a particularly good job, by all accounts. Outsourced clients were unhappy with a lack of innovation and an inability to deliver. Some had taken their IT in-house again in an attempt to drive down costs. IBM SA's global contribution had diminished substantially. I had to try to staunch the bleeding, and sweet-talk disgruntled clients such as the City of Johannesburg, who felt they weren't getting much bang for their buck. I held face-to-face meetings to reassure customers that service would improve under a new team. A key team member was Chris Kelway, a born salesman who had been promoted to an executive position – in my view, a completely wasted resource. He was charming, convincing and convivial. Thanks to Chris, SABMiller became one of our top 100 global accounts and we signed up Safmarine to a ten-year contract and did a deal with Gold Fields. The contracts were part of $385 million (R2,6 billion at the time) in new business brought in in 2006.

Another big IT project brewing at this time was the rolling out of fixed broadband networks to cities. Ekurhuleni on the East Rand was one of the first councils to explore this, not only for the benefit of its two-and-a-half million citizens, but also for surrounding industry and OR Tambo International Airport. Knowing they didn't have the capacity to do it, we approached the city's chief information officer, Nilesh Singh, with an offer to help. I consulted with my boss, General Manager for Global Technology Services Bruce Ross, and a team came out from the UK to hold workshops with Ekurhuleni Metro's ICT department and to explore ways in which municipal broadband could be a source of revenue. For example, they would be able to reduce their reliance on Telkom, to which they were paying more than R4 million a month. The plan was to install subscriber units at pay points, clinics, fire stations and municipal offices.

At the end of the process, Ekurhuleni put together a request for companies interested in bidding for the tender. Having done all the groundwork, we saw this as a mere formality and submitted a proposal to supply them with a Multi Protocol Label Switch (MPLS) network for R35 million. Andile Mbulawa headed up our public sector team and felt confident that we had the tender in the bag.

But after the adjudication process in early 2007, Andile was told that IBM had to partner with a local company, Technology Corporate Management (TCM). At that advanced stage, it made no financial sense to factor in another company, particularly one we hadn't vetted. Andile wasn't sure how to handle it and sought my advice. As far as I was concerned, if our proposal had won there was no need for us to include a local partner. I went to meet Nilesh Singh and explained our position: we had invested significantly already; we had Cisco gold certification, which meant we had the international qualifications and, furthermore, we knew we were the only company capable of delivering on time. If they'd told us from the start they wanted us to partner with someone, we'd have submitted a very different proposal. Something smelled fishy, I thought.

I wasn't surprised when we received a letter from Ekurhuleni saying thanks, but no thanks. TCM was awarded the tender, although at the time it wasn't even certified to implement the Cisco solutions. Andile was gutted, and resigned. He had spent a year working on the deal; I think he felt I had scuppered it in one meeting. Mark Harris, too, thought I had screwed up. It was seen as a failed pitch, an opportunity lost, and generated much internal debate at IBM Europe. Some felt we should go the legal route, because we would win in court. I didn't think it was worth a prolonged legal challenge. I convinced Bruce Ross that some wars aren't worth fighting.

Years later, it came out that there had been something untoward with certain aspects of the broadband deal. The municipality had also awarded a tender for the supply, delivery installation, implementation of computers and components to a company named Meropa, owned by Velero David, who was related through marriage to Nilesh Singh. Suspicions were that there had been bid rigging.

Although not connected to TCM, I was glad we hadn't got involved.

On Sunday, 17 July 2011, SA *Government News Agency*, in an article entitled 'Ex-Ekurhuleni employees appear in court', reported:

> Pretoria – Two former Ekurhuleni employees appeared in court on Friday on charges of fraud involving a R32 million IT tender issued by the city to Meropa Sechabeng Technology in 2008.
>
> The Hawks arrested the two, along with a local businessman, on Thursday morning.
>
> Velero David, Owner of Meropa; Nilesh Singh, former Executive Director of ICT Department and Andrew Mphushomadi, former Chief IT Architect (both in the City of Ekurhuleni) were all charged with fraud and corruption.

*

At the end of 2007 we did a major outsourcing deal with MTN, whereby core functions of its IT management would be transferred to IBM. Mark Harris and Sifiso Dabengwa from MTN led the talks. I knew Sifiso from Wits Business School, where we'd done some MBA classes together. He's impressive: a strategic thinker able to implement his vision. He would, I'd always thought, make a good mentor. In years to come, our paths would cross again.

On 28 January 2008, *IOL* carried an article headed 'IBM scoops contract with MTN':

> Johannesburg – MTN South Africa has outsourced its information systems division, which looks after its technology services, to US technology group IBM.
>
> The companies would not reveal the value of the deal, which is rumoured to be worth an estimated R1 billion.
>
> MTN said yesterday that the decision to outsource the division was, among other things, to improve its own business performance.
>
> The deal was not exclusive and MTN would continue to engage with other service providers when appropriate and to the benefit of its clients.

The deal contributed towards my winning another IBM Global Circle top performer award, honouring the top one per cent of the sales force. This time the trip was to Bermuda, an Atlantic Ocean island off the coast of North Carolina. I was amused when someone noted that at the first Golden Circle event in 1937, people had stayed in tents in Endicott, the birthplace of

IBM, near New York, while in 2008 we had luxury treatment in a territory with the highest GDP per capita in the world.

At the ceremony, Zoleka and I were placed next to Ginni Rometty, who became IBM president and CEO in 2012, the first woman to be appointed to the position. Ginni would go on to prioritise Africa as the next new frontier for growth and, in 2013, she hosted the IBM CIO Leadership Exchange in Joburg. We found her warm and very interested in South Africa.

The accolades I received were a culmination of a turnaround strategy that involved the grass roots of IBM Global Services in South Africa. Traditionally, only sales teams were rewarded and recognised for attaining targets. I had negotiated with Bruce Ross to stretch targets of ten per cent above the plan. The agreement was that the entire IBM South Africa Global Services team would be recognised if we exceeded this stretch target. Throughout the financial year we kept our employees up to date about our performance and in which areas we needed support. Our employees were fully engaged and went out of their way to deliver exceptional service to both internal and external customers.

We also ran a monthly pulse survey within the division to identify any sticky issues, which were then immediately addressed. Motivation within IBM Global Services was at an all-time high. At the end of the financial year we had exceeded our financial targets by fifteen per cent, well above the stretch target. We took staff to Sun City for a packed three days away to celebrate the achievement. This approach to employee recognition was a first for IBM South Africa and one I would replicate in all my future CEO roles. Employee engagement is a source of sustainable competitive advantage.

*

It was becoming clear to me that Mark Harris wasn't going to vacate his job as country general manager any time soon, which left me wondering what to do next. I turned to Marc Lautenbach at IBM HQ. He hooked me up with the senior vice president of global technology services, Mike Daniels, and after a series of conference calls it was decided that I should move to Armonk, New York, to join the strategy division focusing on emerging markets. It was just before the global financial crisis; developed countries weren't doing well and there was huge growth potential in Africa. I'd been trained at Yale to make an impact – now was my chance. But I had niggling doubts.

Politically, the writing was on the wall for Mbeki, and former Deputy President Jacob Zuma's star was ascending. The idea of him taking over the presidency didn't sit well with me. I'd been pretty vocal about the direction the ANC was taking in a series of articles in the press; now I was planning to leave again, instead of staying to help business in what I was sure was going to be a rocky period. Also, my family was settled again. While we were living in France, Zoleka and I had bought a house at Dainfern in northern Joburg. We liked the idea of living in a secure residential estate. Anda could walk to and from school at Dainfern College. Not having high walls between you and your neighbours makes it easier to interact – granted not with ordinary South Africans, but with an interesting community from all over the world.

But Zoleka and Anda were excited by the prospect of exploring the world again and we made plans to move to New York by September of 2008. Dainfern College was disappointed: Anda was a straight-A student, but they wished her well and we made it clear it wouldn't be forever, although we actually envisaged her completing her schooling in the US.

In May, just months before our move, I was approached by an executive search agency. Mindcor's Graham Utian and Winky Ringo told me that Microsoft's Middle East and Africa (MEA) division needed a managing director for its South African operation. Microsoft was a direct competitor to IBM and I felt it inappropriate to even be talking to them. I explained that I was in the process of relocating to the US. Our house was already up for sale.

They disappeared for two months, then Astrid Warren, Microsoft's HR director, came back stronger. Microsoft SA was in trouble. It needed leadership. Cabinet had approved an open-source policy and all government departments would be getting rid of widely used Microsoft Windows desktop programs that came with licences, in the interests of promoting competitiveness and innovation. Open-source software could be shared by many users without a need for a licence and would reduce dependency on imports. The word was out to buy anything *but* Microsoft. Customer satisfaction was at the lowest level in the corporate sector. The leadership team in South Africa seemed at a loss on how to handle this crisis. My interest was piqued; I sniffed a challenge.

I had a family indaba with Zoleka and Anda, who couldn't understand why I was even entertaining these discussions when we'd made up our minds. The truth was that I hadn't really made up my mind. The new South Africa was an experiment that had to work, despite Zuma or whoever was to come, and I wanted to help it work. What I'd learned at Yale needed to be applied in my own country.

Microsoft flew me to the UK for an assessment. It was rigorous: for two days I was subjected to interviews and tests and processes that examined my ability to think strategically. Having got through that, Ali Faramawy, corporate vice president for MEA, flew to South Africa to interview me. I was nervous: being softly spoken is sometimes interpreted as not having enough courage for a top job. Microsoft's CEO at the time was Steve Ballmer, a loud-mouthed American. Ali, an Egyptian who was based in Turkey at the time, made it clear that Microsoft was a diverse organisation and didn't necessarily need larger-than-life personalities. What they needed was someone who could make Microsoft relevant to South Africa, who could refocus the operating style to serving customers, business partners and society – exactly what the Yale World Fellows Program had taught us. Something went zing in my head: I was sold.

My next interview was a conference call with Ali's boss, the president of Microsoft International, Jean-Philippe Courtois. I was at an IBM strategy session at Sun City, so it was awkward to say the least. I had to furtively rush off to my room for an hour to take the call.

I was eventually appointed as managing director of Microsoft South Africa and began undoing already laid personal plans.

27 July 2008

Dear Mrs Ferreira,

I am writing this letter to update you about Anda's pending move to the US. IBM is planning to send us on international assignment at IBM Headquarters in New York.

However, I have subsequently been approached by Microsoft with an offer to head their South African operation.

My family has chosen to accept this offer as we were moving to the US reluctantly.

We informed Deidre about our decision and she has indicated that Dainfern College would gladly accept Anda back.

We are happy and appreciative . . .

I resigned from IBM on 1 August 2008, on the day Mark Harris was leaving for a business trip to Brazil. He was already at the airport. I handed in my notice to HR director Cathy Smith. It was difficult. My replacement, Bill LaFontaine, had already arrived from the US, I had briefed him and welcomed him. Now I was off to work for the competitor. In a tizz, Cathy phoned the whole company and ruined Mark's Brazil trip. I had calls from Bruce Ross and others who had pulled strings to get me the posting in the US. I explained to them that I couldn't hang around forever waiting for the job I really wanted and for which they were supposedly preparing me.

Then, as is customary at IBM when you leave to work for a competitor, I was escorted out of the building and that was that.

Six months into my job at Microsoft, I had a telephone call from Steve Cowley, then general manager of Central and Eastern

Europe, Middle East and Africa. He said: 'We would like you to lead IBM South Africa.' They were trying to recruit me behind Mark's back, with him still in the position. I declined; I had made a commitment to Microsoft to stay for at least five years.

I was leading a company with shrinking business, gaping vacancies and a pariah status that needed to be shed. I would not trade this challenge for anything in the world.

My relationship with Mteto goes back 21 years. On my return from an assignment in France in 1997 with IBM EMEA, to assume the position of sales director for IBM South Africa, I was handed the mandate to manage a number of underperforming sales business units. The telecommunications and industrial businesses needed to be refocused to drive sales growth. Having decided to undertake a strategic initiative to transform the approach to IBM's partnership within a number of key accounts, and conducting assessments of the existing leadership, I decided to find new leadership talent.

I met Mteto, an account executive at the time, who presented to me the strategy of one of the key accounts. I was very impressed with the quality of his work and asked him to manage a project that looked at that entire industry. His outputs were beyond my expectation as they incorporated deep insights and a clear action plan to improve the IBM business in that industry.

Leadership in a multinational company requires strong communications skills, forthright management styles, personal business drive and organisational development. Mteto was a very humble individual and was very quiet in his approach but he demonstrated an intellectual capability that clearly showed his talents.

I decided to appoint Mteto as the telecommunications sector executive. I was surprised at his reaction; he frankly asked me why I thought he was the right man to do the job and he did not immediately jump at the opportunity. I was unaware that another executive had also identified his potential and was trying to entice him to join our services business unit, although it did not match the seniority of the position that I had proposed. After further conversations, Mteto agreed to accept my proposal, on the provision that I fully supported him and helped him to develop the requisite leadership skills.

IBM was invited by Mandela to join a delegation to the US to further business collaboration. While I would have loved to participate, it was an ideal opportunity for Mteto to engage and build a relationship at senior government levels. He left a mark, as Mandela afterwards remarked, 'Look after my homeboy with the white socks.' Mteto quickly stopped his habit of wearing white socks to work!

Needless to say, Mteto dramatically improved the businesses that he was leading. He also developed a strong team around him and was resolute about his personal appointments even though we often differed on his choices. I quickly developed a huge respect for his newly found managerial capability.

My personal ambition was to challenge Mteto to achieve his ultimate potential. IBM had a programme called Nextgen where I was required to identify an employee – someone who had the potential to be developed and promoted through the ranks to a global executive position. Naturally I selected Mteto – who was also a role model for all black professionals – now well on his way to achieving his ultimate potential. Though now I do believe that he is a person who sees this as a perpetual path as opposed to a destination.

Top: Embekweni Store in Tabase, where I learnt from my mother about respecting customers and employees.

Above left: My parents' graves.

Above right: Vandalism at the old family home in Tabase.

Top left: Closing the Tabase chapter is painful.

Top right: A white elephant in Tabase. Lessons learnt.

Above: The Afrox rookies: Ruth Stenhouse Smith and me with our mentor Dave Bawden.

Opposite top: Our first house in Jukskei Park, Joburg, from where we had to forcibly evict our tenants. Now it's a dentist practice.

Opposite bottom: For four years we called 70 Grande Rue Feucherolles, near Paris, home.

58
DENTIST
Reception

70

Right: The Yale Fellows Program built lasting relationships. Zoleka, on the left, with partners of fellows from Philippines, India and Iran.

Middle: Malawian Paul Kwengwere and I used the Yale programme as an opportunity to deliver an 'Africa rising' message.

Bottom: Receiving good corporate citizen recognition from former President Thabo Mbeki, on behalf of IBM SA.

Opposite top: Kabelo Makwane and I took Microsoft SA closer to government by opening an office in Pretoria.

Middle: With Kabelo Makwane, dressed up for one of Microsoft SA's year-end parties.

Bottom: A group of Yale Fellows, representing eighteen countries, who shaped each other's thinking on global issues. I'm to the left of the man holding the bulldog, Yale's mascot.

Above: Microsoft made a commitment to support these small black-owned companies for seven years.

Middle: At the Microsoft SA BEE launch with government representatives Dina Pule, Minister of Communications on the right, and Deputy Minister of Trade and Industry, Maria Ntuli.

Right: The Microsoft BEE deal wouldn't have happened without the support of the DTI's Mvuzo Mtyhobile and Sipho Zikode.

Left: Anda and me at the opening match of the FIFA World Cup in 2010.

Middle: Microsoft SA leadership team after being named 'Best Employer in SA'.

Below: Microsoft SA employees building a house for those less fortunate.

Top: There's nothing better than being recognised by your own: with Mzwanele Manyi and Bonang Mohale at the Black Management Forum's Manager of the Year Award, 2012.

Above: Family holiday in Thailand.

Left: Saying goodbye to Microsoft's Ali Faramawy.

Below: Signing a recognition agreement with the CWU, after MTN's crippling strike in 2015.

Top: Attending a gala dinner hosted by President Zuma to welcome US President Obama and his wife to South Africa.

Above: Work should be fun too. Chester Missing and Conrad Koch keep us entertained at an MTN function.

Left: Zoleka with Anda after receiving her Dainfern College red blazer, the highest award.

Middle: With my brothers and sisters in Mthatha. From left to right – me, Fundile, Pelokazi and Langa.

Bottom: Reconnecting with my sister, Mary Nyati, in London.

Above: Addressing MTN staff on my last day – an emotional moment for me.

Right: But the cake was perfect.

Top left: With Altron founder Dr Bill Venter.

Top right: Conferring with former Public Protector, Thuli Madonsela.

Above: Altron group executives at the 2018 Kick Off.

Top: At the Johannesburg Stock Exchange.

Above: With Bruce Whitfield on his ShapeShifter show.

Top: The new Altron.

Above left: Launching the new Altron brand.

Above right: Explaining to President Ramaphosa why I moved to Altron. He'd been involved in my recruitment to MTN.

Top left: Zoleka and I dressed up for a cousin's wedding in the Eastern Cape.

Top right: My daughters, Azola and Anda.

Above: Sky Tower, Auckland, New Zealand, with Anda and Zoleka.

After a number of promotions, Mteto was granted an assignment internationally to expose him to the global executives and for his own personal development. It was no surprise to me that he excelled on assignment and quickly built a strong personal brand as an IBM leader. He was then appointed as one of the first South Africans to become a global director.

Just before his assignment was due to end, I needed a senior leader to run the African services business, which was the largest IBM business in Africa. Although the global services executives wanted to appoint a leader with strong services skills, I decided that Mteto was the right leader to fill this position. We did however continue to debate his leadership appointments, but by then I realised that while I could express my opinion, he would make his own appointments to achieve his objectives. He continued to deliver the business results in an environment where he had to develop skills in a new discipline and quickly overcame the scepticism of the global services business.

After a few years, Mteto was confronted with the next phase of his career. There were two choices: he was either to succeed me as IBM South Africa general manager, or embark on another assignment for corporate exposure and further development. The decision was to obtain an assignment for him in the US, as this would give him the advantages of working in the global corporation. When he chose instead to join Microsoft as the country general manager, I felt disappointed that we were losing him from the employ of IBM, but inwardly was delighted, as I knew he was well equipped to make a difference on any platform he chose.

– Mark Harris is Independent Director at Pepkor and African Bank

Chapter 7

Windows into BEE

Humans and the unique quality we call empathy . . . will become ever more valuable in a world where the torrent of technology will disrupt the status quo like never before.
— *Satya Nadella, Microsoft CEO*

When I was about six or seven years old I heard raised voices coming from the room where some of my older siblings slept. I wandered in. They were all in there, having a meeting of some sort, but I couldn't understand what it was about because they were talking in English. The atmosphere was tense. One of my sisters told me to 'phuma' (get out).

I thought she was joking and asked: 'Ngoba?' (Why?)

She said sharply: 'Phuma! Ngoba awuzalwa nathi!' (Get out! Because you're not one of us.)

I left, confused, and went to find my mother. I asked her why my sister had said that. She explained that sometimes there was friction in our household because my older siblings weren't her children. They came from another mother and didn't always agree with the way things were run. Noting my confusion, she reassured me that they were my family even though they didn't share her blood. There were, she said, more things that were the same about them and me than were different. We had the same father; the same surname and lived in the same house. It was my first inkling that there could be differences and similarities in one unit and it shaped by views about diversity and inclusion.

The incident remained with me and I related it at a leadership strategy session a few months into my tenure as Microsoft MD. In sharing this personal story with the fifteen-member leadership team, I made it clear how important it was to find commonalities and to make them, not the differences, the foundation. It relaxed the stiff start such interactive conferences often have and lifted the discussion to another level. My colleagues began to open up about their issues with a company they felt loyal to, but which they thought had lost its way. They wanted Microsoft to be more relevant to what was going on in their country, but government's open-source policy and the perceived hostility that came with it had hit them hard. They seemed anxious and confused.

As IBM had done, Microsoft suffered from image issues. When he took over the reins from Steve Ballmer in 2014, Microsoft's third CEO, Satya Nadella, took a dig at a corporate culture in which 'everyone felt the need to be the smartest person in the room', a possible reference to founder Bill Gates, who had created the company in his image. Microsoft's arrogant dominance, so prevalent in the '80s and '90s, no longer attracted customers.

It was a problem that even we in an emerging market felt, and it affected employees. Microsoft SA had an attrition rate of 29 per cent. The previous local MD, Pfungwa Serima, had lasted only two years before 'resigning'. Just before I joined, six members of the leadership team had left at the same time. The company was rudderless.

Serima had left at the end of June 2008 and Fernando de Sousa from the Turkey office had acted as MD. Now, as I listened to my colleagues, I realised there were a few things I would have to 'de-Fernando'– for example, the plan to build a boma to be used for inducting new employees. I found out who was driving it and suggested we find other ways to boost flagging staff morale.

The boma idea reminded me of Nampak in the early '90s. Consultants such as Lovemore Mbigi used to preach the concept of creating an African village in a work environment. These concepts appealed to the politically correct, but in practice they were inherently divisive. Coloureds, Indians and whites almost always quietly undermined such initiatives. I was hellbent on avoiding a path to nowhere. My priority was to make Microsoft relevant to South Africa. This meant aligning our business strategy with the priorities of the country. We couldn't exist in a bubble. We needed to step out of our bomas.

In September 2008, in an article headed 'Microsoft's Man with a Mission', *IT Web* had described my appointment as 'the most controversial since the US software giant opened its doors here'.

> It is the first day of spring and the first day on the job for Microsoft's new country head, Mteto Nyati . . . the first black South African head . . . Unlike many executives in the ICT sector who are inclined to keep their political feelings and observations under wraps, Nyati openly stepped into the political arena when an article written by him about the ANC leadership race was published in the *Sunday Times* . . .

I didn't think I'd overstepped the mark, but I had nailed my colours to the mast the previous year, writing in the *Sunday Times* that populism had ruined South Africa and that we had to stay the current economic course to be a winning nation. I believed that giving Mbeki a third term as ANC president would enable him to protect the policy he'd set in motion and allow the new president of the country to focus on service delivery. The fact that the ANC was muzzling the succession debate, I'd written, allowed opportunists and those with questionable agendas to thrive. Zuma's open campaigning to be the next president meant that potential candidates such as Cyril Ramaphosa were shackled by ANC tradition.

Zuma was elected ANC president in December 2007 and, as I subsequently told *IT Web*, business had to adapt:

> Company executives . . . have to look at the environment in which they operate. The results of the Polokwane conference show that service delivery is the critical factor and the new leadership is under a lot of pressure to deliver services. This is an area where Microsoft can help.

The leadership team and I identified strategic pillars. The most important of these was to shed the image of a multinational in a host country to make money, exploit locals and give back little. One way of becoming relevant, I thought, would be to properly introduce broad-based black economic empowerment by means of a well-thought-out equity equivalent programme – an accepted alternative for multinationals to selling any shareholding in their South African-based companies. Within Microsoft there was a fear of BEE. It was seen as a threat not an opportunity, largely because it wasn't understood. Like many multinationals, Microsoft had tried to skirt around the issue rather than tackle it head on and make it work for all. The company wasn't even BEE compliant.

Kethan Parbhoo, a sales manager in the public sector, was seconded to my office to become my business manager. He was a high performer and was regarded as top talent. Together we crafted our BEE strategy. At Yale I had written articles about the long-term dangers of giving black people unearned minority equity in white-owned companies. I felt that this so-called economic empowerment reduced blacks to beggars and parasites, effectively undermining self-development. I preached entrepreneurship as the best way of lifting any nation out of poverty.

As a country, we are surrounded by societal problems screaming for solutions. Instead of cursing these problems we should relish the opportunity to solve them. It was against this backdrop that Kethan and I formulated the new BEE strategy for Microsoft. Our company gave us the opportunity to walk the talk. We embraced the challenge.

Our first task though was to demystify BEE within Microsoft SA. To many minority groups, BEE or transformation meant exclusion. This 'not for us' perception was one I wanted to address directly. We had to get all employees enthused about what we were going to do.

We held a town-hall-type meeting at our Bryanston headquarters and unpacked the BEE scorecard to our 450-odd staff members. Back then the scorecard had seven elements: ownership, twenty points; management control, ten points; employment

134

equity, fifteen points; skills development, fifteen; preferential procurement, twenty; enterprise development, fifteen and socio-economic development, five points.

At the meeting, it was evident that most fears revolved around employment equity. We made it clear that instead of getting rid of people, we would change the demographics within Microsoft SA by growing our business. We reassured staff members that we needed their expertise. I asked for two things from them: their commitment to grow our business, and diversity. I appealed to managers to hire people who were different from them, be it through race, gender or age. For example, if a manager happened to be a white 'baby boomer' male, we expected him to hire blacks, millennials or white women.

Once we'd mapped out how we were going to get full ownership points through our equity equivalent programme, we began to see buy in and excitement. Generally BEE programmes are divisive – ours was exactly the opposite. All our employees had a role to play in making Microsoft locally relevant. The South African constitution says our country belongs to all who live in it.

When I was at Yale I had pondered BEE. Wouldn't it be better to create a new model for entrepreneurship by investing in black enterprises and setting a benchmark for developing talent? I wanted to put my ideas into practice. If we could plough 25 per cent of Microsoft SA's worth – about half a billion rand – into the local software industry, there could be many winners. We could empower small IT companies to provide solutions for sectors across health, security and education. We just had to work out how. And find an executive sponsor.

In 2009 I attended a PRISM (Priority Setting Meeting) at Microsoft HQ in Redmond, near Seattle. There I introduced myself to Orlando Ayala, an advisor to Microsoft Chief Operations Officer Kevin Turner. As a Colombian, Orlando had a good grasp of the challenges I was facing: his home country and mine were grappling with similar political and socio-economic issues. I told him about my envisaged BEE project and asked him if he would consider being our executive sponsor. He said he would, but that he would first have to travel to South Africa to gain an understanding of the local environment. During his visit, we met Nomonde Mesatywa and Mvuzo Mtyhobile, BEE directors in the Department of Trade and Industry (DTI), who explained to him the concept of BEE and the various approaches to complying with the law.

Orlando agreed to be our Redmond ambassador and to help us seek the Microsoft global funding – $75 million – to support black software development and African innovation.

The deal hit home.

> In one of the biggest equity equivalent deals seen in South Africa to date, Microsoft is to invest almost half a billion rand over the next seven years into the local software industry. – IT *News Africa*
>
> Arthur Goldstuck, the managing director of technology research house World Wide Worx, welcomed the deal as a significant step for BEE in the technology industry.
>
> 'This is the first time a major multinational is willing to put both financial muscle and expertise behind the growth of the SME sector, as opposed to a generic offering of money that is not applied to a specific outcome,' said Goldstuck.

The process kicks off on 28 April 2010 with the issuing of the nationwide RFP, inviting black-owned software development companies to apply. – *My Broadband*

Microsoft South Africa managing director Mteto Nyati said the investment would directly address some of the key challenges facing the government and South Africa as a whole – namely creating jobs, developing enterprises, building the local software economy and developing scarce technology skills. – *Mail & Guardian*

But nothing is simple when dealing with government. Although we had consulted with the DTI, when it came to implementation there was pushback from both Nomonde and Mvuzo. We had divergent views about BEE. They felt that multinationals should not be exempt from selling 25 per cent equity to black people. They didn't like or support the equity equivalent programme and did everything possible to frustrate our efforts. I decided to escalate the issue to the director-general, Tshediso Matona. Some years later, he was to spend a turbulent five months as Eskom CEO before being dumped by the board because he didn't fit with 'plans' – i.e. looting.

Although no one had done BEE like this before, he thought our strategy was sound and gave us the go-ahead to begin finding our innovators, who had to be majority black-owned software developers with a maximum of 30 full-time employees and a turnover of no more than R10 million per annum. His only issue was the number of local partners we were planning to support. Our strategy called for a maximum of eight small black-owned businesses. The DTI felt we should support over a hundred black enterprises. We explained the logic of not spreading ourselves too thin and the power of focus. Tshediso bought our approach and became an enthusiastic supporter of our model.

We advertised on radio and TV, calling for companies who felt they had developed something attractive to the rest of the world. The print advert was a picture of a young black man in an empty room, save for four lonely boxes on the floor. Around him, stretching up to the roof, were stencilled sketches of many more boxes towering to the ceiling, obviously alluding to his aspirations. In the foreground was the outline of a white computer geek, ready to assist. The ad read:

> We see things not as they are, but as they could be.
>
> As South Africans, we dream of the future.
>
> Of something bigger.
>
> Of something better.
>
> At Microsoft, we believe in that dream. Which is why from April this year, we're investing heavily in building black-owned software companies of the future.
>
> It is just part of our commitment to South Africa. And it is just part of our drive to turn dreams into reality.

The campaign bore fruit – we received close to 700 applications. Once we had whittled down the list – removing chancers and fronters – to 50, then to single figures, we put in place business plans and found mentors within Microsoft. Once again Microsofties of all backgrounds came to the party, volunteering their time and expertise. This was BEE with a difference and I felt proud of it. As a country we can do much if we rise above petty differences and focus on what we share – our humanity.

Government red tape delayed the implementation by nearly a year. There were differences over the funding model. The DTI wanted to ring-fence the entire amount upfront. As we were funding the deal locally, it would have crippled us. We eventually compromised: we would invest on an annual basis in line with a jointly agreed business plan. And they would audit us accordingly, to ensure we had invested the four per cent of total revenue that would earn us the 20 points needed to take us to BEE level 2.

Deputy DG of Trade and Industry Sipho Zikode described it as the most challenging equity equivalent programme they'd ever had to deal with.

Three months before the much-anticipated launch, we sent an invitation to the incumbent president of South Africa, Jacob Zuma. During their respective presidential terms, Mandela and Mbeki had regularly met business leaders to ensure a sound plan was being developed for the economic wellbeing of the country. But we never heard a word from Zuma's office and on the day of our function in March 2011, he instead went to congratulate Mamelodi Sundowns soccer team on winning the Premier League. Perhaps he was ill advised; perhaps he was simply anti-business. We will never know.

Ali Faramawy came out from Turkey. We asked comedian and political commentator Trevor Noah to be the MC for the BEE launch event. He was in top form. He had a go at everybody and we laughed our lungs out. This is how I like to do things – trying to make sure that work is fun. I introduced our first four group empowerment partners to the media and to the DTI:

One of the companies chosen was BUI, which provided software security and services to banks, the police and the justice department. It had 18 staffers with branches in Joburg and Cape Town.

There was a Durban-based company called Home Grown Business Integrations, which created cloud-based software to boost government delivery to rural people. It had six staff members and had designed a prepaid electricity open-platform solution for municipalities.

Cape-based Maxxor developed custom software and consumer applications on the Microsoft platform for mobile phones, while the Pietermaritzburg-based Chillisoft developed software for the healthcare sector and parastatals, specifically to alleviate service delivery bottlenecks.

In my media statement, I committed Microsoft to growing more young black companies:

On 21 March 2011, *IT Week*'s article, entitled 'Mteto Nyati leads Microsoft into new era', read:

> Microsoft faced an uphill battle to get its empowerment equity plan approved by the Department of Trade and Industry (DTI), but the company's victory has changed the face of transformation in South Africa.
>
> The software giant has now joined an exclusive club – becoming one of only a handful of multinationals that have invested in empowerment deals.
>
> Microsoft's empowerment plan is groundbreaking – creating a new model for transformation never before seen in South Africa. It could pave the way for more investments into the empowerment economy, worth around R40 billion across all the country's sectors.

Eight months later we announced that Mmapro IT Solutions and iSolv Technologies had also joined the Microsoft BEE partner network. iSolv has since become a global IT company, providing leading-edge solutions to their international customers, and BUI has been acquired by First Technology.

I was proud of the positive results of this initiative and the way it had been received. On 5 November 2011, an article entitled 'A window into best practice' appeared in *City Press*:

> Mteto Nyati . . . is an unassuming and softly spoken man whom you would easily pass over as just one of the . . . employees at the organisation's headquarters in northern Joburg.
>
> Just as [Bill] Gates was in the early days of personal computers,

Nyati is a pioneering business and leadership thinker in the age of economic empowerment . . .

It was through a pioneering and innovative black economic empowerment deal that Nyati stamped his mark on local business thinking.

In April, Nyati led Microsoft SA to go against the grain and produced the form of economic empowerment that is radically different from what had been seen here before.

Unlike the path many multinationals and historically white-owned companies have taken, the name or political party membership of the beneficiary was irrelevant.

Not everyone was happy. Microsoft's traditional local IT partners, most of whom were white, felt they were being discriminated against. One of my most vocal critics was Greg Mahlknecht, the founder of Always Active Technologies.

Some years later, when I surprised IT professionals and analysts by leaving MTN South Africa to join the Altron Group, Greg's contribution to an online discussion arising from the announcement on *Tech Central*, was:

[. . .] Nyati was a disappointment at Microsoft – anyone who had the misfortune of dealing with Microsoft SA during his reign will know this. I haven't seen any signs of turnaround at MTN – its reputation is as bad as ever, if not worse . . .

In its heyday, Altron was a very engineering-driven company; when I was at varsity in the early '90s, UEC was one of the best bursaries to get, and a number of my friends worked there; I feel that's where the wheels fell off the company – when the engineering took a back seat and the suits took over. Nyati might be a mechanical [*sic*] engineer, but he has no experience in the electronic/manufacturing sector so will have that year dead period while he learns the industry – something that Altron cannot afford. This appointment puzzles me.

In my opinion, Greg represents a small, but vocal group of white South Africans who associate black leadership with corruption, incompetence and laziness. They don't have the burden of presenting facts like the rest of us. Their colour gives them permission to destroy careers. This is what I have come to know as white privilege. The playing fields are never level. One can be angry about it, or weep about it. I don't waste my emotions on bigots. I just try to outperform racists. I subscribe to former US first lady Michelle Obama's adage – 'When they go low, we go high'.

Every day, I wake up to face big challenges in the corporate world, motivated by the Gregs of this world. The least I can give them is cognitive dissonance – a bit of discomfort to challenge their cherished belief systems. They deserve that gift from darkies.

*

In his 2017 book *Hit Refresh: The Quest to Rediscover Microsoft's Soul and Imagine a Better Future for Everyone*, Satya Nadella wrote about disrupting Microsoft's culture and changing the style of communication from one that was top-down to one that was more collaborative. He observed that bureaucracy and internal politics were dominating, instead of innovation and teamwork. I also had a lot of respect for Satya's predecessor, Steve

Ballmer, who was a visionary in many ways. He had, for example, steered the shift from desktop to data centres and the introduction of cloud computing. However, during his time at the helm, new ideas were often trapped because employees never came out of their silos to talk to each other.

It was a syndrome I was all too familiar with at Microsoft SA – one I chose to address in a rather unusual way. To get staff more involved in the company, I held monthly lunch sessions with employees called 'Roundtable!' Managers were excluded, so staff could openly discuss their problems and concerns. I'd leave my PA, Shenaaz Aliverdi, behind, take a notebook with me and ask questions like: what would you do differently if you were me? What is it that management is doing right and should do more of? Participants had to answer both questions – they couldn't be passive. You'd be amazed at the insights one gets about business from these two questions.

The trick, I find, when having these discussions is to act on suggestions and to attribute change directly to those who initiate ideas. Otherwise it's a waste of time. Some staffers wished their managers would go on the road with them and feel their pain when dealing with customers; others wanted to directly influence the direction of the company and needed more recognition for closing deals.

I also initiated monthly company meetings. Colleagues based in locations such as Cape Town, Durban and Port Elizabeth connected via videoconferencing – the technology that we were selling to our customers. Microsofties were drinking their own champagne.

These monthly meetings were famous for their candour.

Against the advice of HR, I introduced a performance barometer that showed which business units were meeting targets and which weren't, directly linking business unit leaders to their work and even including a photograph of them. HR seemed to think non-performers might feel discouraged. I was fine with that.

Non-performing businesses could not be orphans. Specific leaders had to be accountable to them. Within a few months, all our businesses turned green, as they should. In no time the entire subsidiary was consistently delivering double-digit revenue and profit growth. We maintained this level of performance for five years in a row. Ali Faramawy and Jean-Philippe Courtois could count on Microsoft SA.

I had once again negotiated with Ali to recognise the entire subsidiary every time we exceeded our full year financial targets. In the first year the team voted to go on a sea cruise from Durban to the Mozambican islands. Head office was nervous – where would Microsoft SA be if the ship sank? We appeased them by making sure there were helicopters on standby in the unlikely event of such a catastrophe and we set off for four days of fun. No work, only play.

I was rather horrified by the amount of extramarital 'playing' that went on below deck. On our return, I organised a survey to find out whether spouses should come along on such trips in future. To my surprise, 55 per cent of staff voted no, 45 per cent were in favour. I'm old-fashioned when it comes to fidelity, so on moral grounds I overruled them. The majority isn't always right. As a leader there are certain issues you need to take a position on.

On the next trip the following year, we included partners and hired a convoy of buses to take us to Legend Golf and Safari Resort in the Waterberg. At the end of the year we held a kiddies' party, also attended by spouses. These events left a lasting impression on families about Microsoft SA and were another reason for employees to choose to stay with us.

Our efforts worked: we began to walk tall and even to receive some recognition.

Deloitte and CRF did annual surveys, looking at the attractiveness of employers and determining employees' engagement with them. Microsoft SA won 'Deloitte Best Company to Work For' and CRF 'Best Employer' two years in a row.

Keeping a company of 450 people happy is no mean feat.

When I'd taken over as MD, we – the biggest subsidiary of the MEA region – had been under-performing with negative revenue and profit growth. But within two years we exceeded budget and grew the business by double digits, in line with expectations from head office. We also doubled our public sector business, partly because we tackled it differently. I appointed Kabelo Makwane, who joined us from Cisco Systems, as public sector director. His approach was solution-centric as opposed to product-pushing. He and his team spent time trying to understand government's pain points. They crafted solutions to help various government departments address service delivery issues, while reducing costs. This is how account managers should approach their work. He showed government a different side to Microsoft: a company that listened, delivered and advocated for the customer. It helped us gain a significant market share within the public sector.

Kabelo worked hard at our relationship with the State Information Technology Agency (SITA) promoting it within government departments – an interesting role reversal. Microsoft became a strategic partner to SITA. We also signed a framework agreement with them that effectively reduced government's cost of computing. This was a masterstroke. Through this agreement, government channelled products that they would, traditionally have bought from competitors. It was a win-win relationship – exactly what we had intended.

We live in a strange country. When I was recruiting Kabelo from Cisco, I had also appointed an acting public sector director, Chris Roberts, a white American. As I've mentioned, it's a South African business tendency to assume that if your customer is government, whoever deals with them on a corporate level must be black. I was surprised by how Chris was embraced by his black government customers. Black public officials were very happy to meet with Chris, but not so much with their black compatriots. How does one explain that? We're a funny bunch. Apartheid legacies live on.

Home Affairs became a customer, as did several other arms of a government that had once declared they would buy anything *but* Microsoft. I had always regarded the perceived hostility with the open-source community as exactly that – a perception – and one that could be changed by getting involved in projects that were relevant.

Globally, Microsoft wasn't doing well, which was disappointing because South Africa was. But we couldn't control external factors. The new Windows 8 operating system hadn't set the industry on fire and had come hot on the heels of the disastrous Windows Vista OS. Nor had Microsoft's partnership with Nokia – designed to penetrate the mobile market and shore up the struggling Windows Phone operating system – taken off. In April 2013, activist investor ValueAct Capital took a $2-billion stake in Microsoft. That was the start of then CEO Steve Ballmer's problems.

In August 2013, he announced his resignation to staff.

> I am writing to let you know that I will retire as CEO of Microsoft within the next 12 months, after a successor is chosen. There is never a perfect time for this type of transition, but now is the right time. My original thoughts on timing would have had my retirement happen in the middle of our transformation to a devices and services company focused on empowering customers in the activities they value most.
>
> We need a CEO who will be here longer term for this new direction. You can read the press release on Microsoft News Center. This is a time of important transformation for Microsoft. Our new Senior Leadership team is amazing. The strategy we have generated is first class. Our new organization, which is centered on functions and engineering areas, is right for the opportunities and challenges ahead.
>
> Microsoft is an amazing place. I love this company. I love the way we helped invent and popularize computing and the PC. I love the bigness and boldness of our bets. I love our people and their talent and our willingness to accept and embrace their range of capabilities, including their quirks. I love the way we embrace and work with other companies to change the world and succeed together. I love the breadth and diversity of our customers, from consumer to enterprise, across industries, countries, and people of all backgrounds and age groups.

I am proud of what we have achieved. We have grown from $7.5 million to nearly $78 billion since I joined Microsoft, and we have grown from employing just over 30 people to almost 100,000. I feel good about playing a role in that success and having committed 100 percent emotionally all the way. We have more than 1 billion users and earn a great profit for our shareholders. We have delivered more profit and cash return to shareholders than virtually any other company in history. I am excited by our mission of empowering the world and believe in our future success.

I cherish my Microsoft ownership, and look forward to continuing as one of Microsoft's largest owners.

This is an emotional and difficult thing for me to do. I take this step in the best interests of the company I love; it is the thing outside of my family and closest friends that matters to me most. Microsoft has all its best days ahead.

Know you are part of the best team in the industry and have the right technology assets. We cannot and will not miss a beat in these transitions. I am focused and driving hard and know I can count on all of you to do the same.

Let's do ourselves proud.

Steve

ValueAct Capital was my first exposure to activist investors – groups that purchase large numbers of shares in order to obtain seats on the board, with a view to effecting major change within a company. It was not to be my last: a few years later I sat across the table from engaged shareholders Value Capital Partners, being interviewed for the position of Altron Group Chief Executive.

*

Back at Microsoft SA we had identified that IT skills shortages were a threat to continued revenue growth. Our partners complained about the quality of technical skills coming through our universities. As a company, we had a choice of joining the chorus of negativity or doing something about it. I have long realised the futility of complaining.

My leadership team and I were surprised that in a society where we have such high youth unemployment, we also have high IT skills shortages. We decided to do an audit of the IT skills our partners were looking for. Once we had established the common skills they needed, we set out to create a programme to develop them and launched 'Student to Business'. We recruited unemployed graduates and trained them up. Over twelve months, we also focused on imparting soft skills to our trainees, and were able to place them in our partner network. We extended the initiative to include partnerships with the South African Local Government Association (SALGA), placing these young people in municipalities that did not have IT staff. They became the saviours of some struggling municipalities. We were transforming lives and doing good – while doing good business.

It was at this time that the newly appointed minister of finance, Pravin Gordhan, announced the Jobs Fund. The objective was for government to co-finance public, private and NGO projects that could contribute to job creation. I challenged Vis Naidoo of the Citizenship Lead division and Microsoft's expert on social issues, to apply for the Jobs Fund. And so Microsoft SA became one of the first companies to partner with government in this project. Over a period of five years we were able to place more than 9 000 unemployed graduates into our partner network and into government. Who said 'white monopoly capital' companies must be destroyed? What does 'white monopoly capital' mean for that matter? We need black and white hands on deck to solve our economic problems. We need big and small companies. We need male and female. We need to focus on urban and rural. We need both the manufacturing and services sectors. It is not an either/or situation. As a nation, we have to understand the power of 'and'. These ideals are deeply embedded in our national constitution. It is who we are.

*

When I started at Microsoft there was no up-and-coming leadership to speak of. So I spoke to Ali Faramawy and got funding for a programme called BOLD – build organisational leadership depth – to train up people to fill executive positions when they became vacant. I brought in Benny Serepong, Kabelo Makwane, Melanie Botha, Zoaib Hoosen and many other diverse leaders through this programme. When I appointed them I was already thinking about my succession slate. They were put through a structured development plan and given stretch projects. Kabelo did a great job turning around our public sector business. Zoaib was responsible for our commercial business. He helped shift our engagement with customers by focusing on line of business. Traditionally, we had engaged IT managers, when in reality IT budgets were increasingly being managed by a line of business executives. Benny, a born salesman, was responsible for our OEM (original equipment manufacturer) business. And Melanie, a fluent speaker of isiZulu – unusual for a white person – was director of consumer channels, driving sales and marketing.

I had an agreement with Ali and Jean-Philippe that I would lead Microsoft SA for five years. Kabelo and Zoaib had emerged as leading candidates for the MD role. We decided to appoint Kabelo as the managing director for Nigeria. Zoaib was appointed as chief operating officer in South Africa. I was asked to do another year, while Zoaib was being monitored in his new role. I began easing myself out of the local operation.

We had accomplished a lot in five years. Microsoft was now seen as a local company focused on addressing the priorities of South Africa. The market was also paying attention. In 2012, the BMF, which was often critical of multinational companies, recognised me as manager of the year and the BMF presidents Mzwanele Manyi and Bonang Mohale presented me with the award.

In June 2013, Barack Obama, accompanied by his family, made his first visit to South Africa as US president. I have always looked up to the Obamas, fascinated by how Barack seems to balance work and family. When I received an invite from the presidency to an exclusive gala dinner hosted by Jacob Zuma, I was over the moon. President Obama was impressive in person. His love for his wife was visible throughout the evening. This was my highlight for 2013.

Later in the year, the Institute of IT Professionals SA (IITPSA) announced Professor Barry Dwolatzky and me as joint winners of ICT Personality of the Year. It was good to be recognised by industry peers for nurturing young talent and emerging entre-preneurs and making that a core principle of our careers.

In 2014 I was appointed general manager for MEA emerging markets. Zoaib became MD of Microsoft South Africa. Business website *BusinessTech* reported:

> Microsoft South Africa announced in a press release on Tuesday, 1 July 2014 that its managing director of six years, Mteto Nyati . . . will be working with leadership teams across MEA to develop and implement growth strategies for the emerging markets within the Middle East and Africa region . . ..
>
> 'Since his appointment to the post a year ago, Zoaib has been managing a large portion of the Microsoft SA business. He is a natural fit as managing director for the business going forward,' Nyati said.

But a few months into my new position, a multibillion-dollar mobile communications company came calling.

MTN Group CEO Sifiso Dabengwa had been knocking on my door for three years. I had not entertained these discussions previously because of my commitment to Ali and Jean-Philippe. Once that had been fulfilled, Sifiso offered me a position that sounded as if it had the potential to go places.

I took a step into the unknown.

From: Ali Faramawy

Sent: Thursday, September 4, 2014 6:24 PM

To: MS MEA

Cc: Jean-Philippe Courtois; Orlando Ayala; Stijn Nauwelaerts

Subject: Mteto moving on . . .

Dear Friends

I am sad to report that Mteto has decided to move. Mteto will join the executive team of a large South African company with again strong African connections and aspirations. I would have loved to see Mteto continue to enjoy his passion for his country and for the continent from within Microsoft but he feels this is the right step for him from both career and personal standpoints.

I cannot thank Mteto enough for all his efforts and support. Great years transforming Microsoft South Africa, and teaching us all a thing or two about leadership, humility, customer focus and love for the continent. Mteto will continue with us till the end of September.

I will not backfill the role that Mteto does for now. The 4Afrika team will go back to reporting to me and I will ask Fernando and Michael Kogeler to team up to help us put together the blue prints for Emerging MEA going forward.

I know this is not the best news to share. Yet I am still proud and fortunate that someone like Mteto was and still will be one of us.

Best Regards

Ali Faramawy
Corporate Vice President
Microsoft | Middle East & Africa

From: Kevin Turner

Sent: Thursday, September 4, 2014 10:34 PM

To: Mteto Nyati

Subject: Thank You

Mteto,

Ali and Jean-Philippe informed me of your decision to accept a new role at MTN.

Since you took the lead for us in South Africa back in 2008 our business has grown more than 60%. I appreciate all you have done to both grow our business and to put an outstanding team in place.

Know that I am available if you need anything in the future. I wish you the best in your new role and please, do stay in touch.

Thank you for all you have done for Microsoft!

kt

Chapter 8

Dead Man Walking

'Union chants "voetsek" to MTN execs'
> – *Fin24Tech*, 20 May 2015

'MTN strike turns chaotic'
> – *Moneyweb*, 29 May 2015

'MTN granted interdict against striking workers'
> – *Biznews*, 13 June 2015

The Communication Workers' Union strike dragged on for the whole of May, June and into July. On 13 July, at possibly the worst time ever, I was appointed CEO of MTN South Africa.

When, nine months earlier, I'd joined MTN as group chief enterprise officer, a journalist had asked me why someone with such high ethics could join such a shady company. The Group had had its fair share of controversy: the alleged manipulation of the Money Mobile platform in Uganda; allegations of bribery in Iran to win a mobile licence there and the diversion of sponsor money for an ICT Indaba, resulting in the suspension of corporate services head Robert Madzonga.

The simple answer was that it was important to me to show that black people were capable of building successful global organisations rooted in good governance. I wanted to be part of a mainly black leadership team that would transform the MTN Group into a world-class digital company and I felt that my experience in working for multinational companies such as IBM and Microsoft would contribute to that. South Africa needed to create and maintain an enabling environment that allowed businesses to thrive. Not by relying on prayers, or sangomas, but through agreeing on a common national agenda. It wasn't easy under Zuma, who seemed intent on stomping on the rule of law and looking on as strong institutions buckled.

I told *City Press*: 'There's a reason why I chose to work for MTN – it has huge potential to touch people in the right way. We may not be using it like that right now, but we can significantly and positively impact this continent in terms of human development.' I was thinking of areas such as healthcare, education, financial inclusion and agriculture.

MTN has 22 operations across Africa and the Middle East, and needed to build and maintain new relationships and sources of revenue in those regions.

When I joined MTN I began visiting operations in Nigeria, Ghana, the Ivory Coast, Botswana and Kenya and discovered that although the company's presence was geographically widespread, head office was surprisingly insular. Staff in those countries told me that, when group executives visited, they hardly ever engaged with employees and customers. This concerned me as my understanding of our role at headquarters implied a high level of involvement: giving operational leadership direction, guiding and coaching staff, reviewing and providing feedback to operating companies and helping with their sales effort – all while holding them accountable for results. MTN head office appeared to operate more as a holding company than as a strong centre.

I proposed to our group CEO, Sifiso Dabengwa, that a solution might be to assign group executives to act as sponsors to strategic enterprise customers. On their visits to our operating companies in various countries, the executives could meet these customers at CxO level, broadening, elevating and strengthening MTN's relationship with them. He liked the idea and we presented it to group exco for discussion and adoption.

My assessment was that, as a team, we were too internally focused. My suggested partnership executive programme would force us to engage customers, and thus gain industry and market insights. I considered this a step in the right direction towards achieving our goal of becoming customer centric.

I had been a Vodacom customer since 1996 and had ported to MTN when I joined the group. The porting process had been laborious, with little feedback or interaction. My family and I had felt irrelevant as customers. As is often the case in monolithic companies, there was little client focus. In the three group executive committee meetings I'd attended, nobody had ever mentioned the customer. We were concerned largely with cost reduction and containment. When Sifiso asked what my first observations of the group were, I gave him this honest feedback. To his credit, he immediately changed the group executive committee agenda to include discussions on customer experience.

There wasn't much engagement with employees either, as illustrated by the protracted strike. MTN was a relatively young company with little experience in labour matters, not having gone through the enormity of industrial action in the '80s. Paul Norman, the group chief human resources officer, regarded the strike as an MTN SA problem, even though it reflected badly on the MTN brand. The strikers' demands – union recognition, bonuses and above inflation salary increments – were issues that could've been thrashed out around a table. I got on with my job, but felt unsettled that as a communications company, we were failing at our own business.

The IT space was realigning and MTN was puffing along behind. Voice revenue was dwindling. My mission was to build new sources of revenue from business as opposed to consumer customers. There had been some poor attempts at venturing into information technology space. MTN had acquired Verizon Business SA and Afrihost. Verizon Business was renamed MTN Business. It was this division that I had to grow. There were two options: to catch up organically, or to acquire an IT services company. Examples of companies that had chosen the latter option were Telkom, which had acquired BCX, and Japan's

Nippon Telegraph and Telephone Corp, which had bought Dimension Data.

After extensive market analysis, I settled on Altron as a possible acquisition target. On their board was an old friend from my MBA class, Jacob Modise, and one of the non-executive directors was Mandela's former justice minister, Penuell Maduna, who'd been Zoleka's boss when she worked at Shell House. I approached Jacob for more insight into the company. He encouraged us to make an offer. I reached out to Altron Chief Executive Robbie Venter to discuss our intentions and seek his guidance on process. He was clear that Altron needed a formal offer. We tabled a non-binding indicative offer, subject to formal technical and financial due diligence. I contracted Accenture and McKinsey to do this over the following four months. At the end of the process I realised that although Altron's technical capabilities were impressive, in particular their Bytes and Altech divisions, it was an ungainly beast, divided into ten operations that functioned largely autonomously. I felt that it would present a business risk to try to integrate these units into MTN, which didn't have a great record at branching out beyond its core telecommunications business – evident from Verizon and Afrihost. I recommended to group exco that we should not proceed with the transaction.

When I informed Robbie about our decision, I could detect his disappointment. As much as I empathised with him, I knew this was the right decision for both of our businesses. On the positive side, the due diligence process gave me valuable insight into Altron – though of course at the time I had no inkling that I would end up leading this iconic South African company.

Back at the MTN ranch, the strike was intensifying. Unused to the robust nature of our industrial action, the CEO of MTN South Africa, Lebanese-born Ahmad Farroukh, wasn't handling it well. He began fearing for his life. Two months into the strike, he resigned.

Business Report's headline on 7 July 2015 was 'Crisis at MTN claims scalp of Farroukh' and the article read:

> MTN South Africa chief executive Ahmad Farroukh yesterday became the first casualty of the worst crisis that has hit the giant cellular company in more than 20 years of operating history in the country.
>
> Farroukh, 54, abruptly resigned yesterday ending months of speculation that he was going owing to the loss of lucrative corporate contracts and a wage strike that had negatively affected services at the country's second largest cellular operator.
>
> MTN insiders yesterday told *Business Report* that Farroukh fell because of the loss the company had suffered after surrendering the market share to rival operators.
>
> The company's shares closed 2,77 per cent down at R227,09.

The next day, *IT Web* reported:

> Following . . . the abrupt departure of its CEO, MTN SA has not disclosed its succession plan, or openly discussed the reasons for Ahmad Farroukh's unexpected resignation.
>
> On Monday, the country's second-largest mobile operator confirmed Farroukh would leave at the end of the month . . . after less than a year in the top position.

An accompanying photograph showed Ahmad reading employees' demands at the start of the strike, with Communication Workers' Union (CWU) President Clyde Mervin and his deputy, Thabo Mogalane, looking on. In the background was a poster: 'Faro – go back to Egypt'.

MTN SA was so obviously handling the strike wrongly that when Sifiso Dabengwa approached me to replace Farroukh, I felt a surge of enthusiasm. I'd learned from Lot Ndlovu during my Afrox days, and at Nampak, that strikes should first of all never be allowed to happen and if they did, they had to end as soon as possible. A company can take a long time to recover from a protracted strike – both financially and morally. At IBM or Microsoft, this situation would never have arisen. But at MTN HQ, we remained strangely detached and buried our heads in the sand as things grew ugly. The police had to be called after striking workers blocked 14th Avenue in Fairland, which leads to the N1.

I asked Sifiso to give me a few days to consider the offer, and I went home to talk to Zoleka. She knew how I felt about the strike and the damage it was doing to the MTN brand. We had watched MTN staffers insulting their leaders on national TV and here I was toying with the idea of replacing Farroukh. Even considering the job seemed madness. My wife knew how invested I was in helping MTN transform into a world-class digital company. I value her input. She's intuitive. We agreed that I had the necessary competences to turn the situation around. We also figured that the challenge would enhance my long-term career plans within the group.

162

Still, I asked myself the sobering question: are the issues faced by MTN South Africa within management control or not? I analysed poor customer experience, as well as poor employee relations, and realised both rested firmly on the shoulders of management. By making different choices, management could dramatically change things. It was at this point that I knew I was in.

While Sifiso sought approval for my appointment from the board, I approached the CWU. There was no way of fixing MTN SA without first resolving the strike. I made it my priority. My brother Fundile knew Sipho Nkese, who had dealt with CWU while working at the Post Office as human resources director. Sipho arranged a face-to-face meeting with Clyde Mervin at the Midrand Protea Hotel. We met twice over that weekend, along with other members of the CWU executive. In principle, we agreed that they would call off the strike as it was damaging to both sides. CWU said it would accept what MTN had offered them before the strike: a four per cent increase. The workers owed the company in terms of pension and benefits and we agreed that this would be deducted from their salaries over a period of time, to ease the pain.

That Sunday, 12 July 2015, I was surprised to read in the *Sunday Times* that my appointment as CEO wasn't a fait accompli. According to the article, under the headline 'MTN Board members keen to see women vying for CEO', the board wanted a female and had someone in mind.

> Insiders say several names have been mooted to head the troubled South African unit permanently. The successful candidate would be the third CEO in two years at MTN SA.

The article, which was clearly not backing me, went on to quote independent non-executive director Dawn Marole saying that Philisiwe Sibiya was being 'groomed for the job' and that was the reason she'd been sent to Cameroon. 'Philisiwe is a very smart woman and competent . . . She is one of the key stars within the group.'

The article went on about Marole's desire to have a woman in this key position and barely mentioned me or the rest of the board members, although she claimed to be speaking on behalf of some of them and said they would be scrutinising the candidate's list: 'If there are no women . . . then we want an explanation on why we couldn't find those women . . . it's an issue that we take seriously at MTN, especially us women on the board.'

The following day I was appointed as CEO of MTN SA. I thanked Sifiso, ignoring Dawn Marole who, incidentally, is my old friend Oupa Magashula's sister. Sifiso introduced me to the executive committee and we got down to the business of resolving the strike. A majority of exco members were against re-engaging the union. They had previously resolved to break the CWU by stretching the strike out as long as possible. The belief was that striking employees wouldn't survive another month with no pay. I had no time for what I saw as a non-strategy. I tasked Themba Nyathi, chief HR officer, and Alpheus Mangale, chief enterprise business officer, to re-open negotiations with the CWU. Separately, I briefed them on the weekend discussions and saw relief in their eyes. In my previous role as group chief enterprise officer I had recruited Alpheus from Cisco, where he'd been managing director. He'd been on my succession slate at Microsoft SA as an external candidate and had been assessed and approved by both Ali Faramawy and Jean-Philippe Courtois. Alpheus is one of the sharpest minds I know. I had also recommended him for a senior and strategic role at Standard Bank. He proceeded to charm CWU, leading us to the next phase of MTN South Africa's turnaround.

On 16 July 2015, three days after my appointment, talk-show host John Robbie interviewed me at 7:48 am on *Talk Radio 702*:

JR: MTN has been a troubled company of late. We've had this strike that's been going on for ages and I know because the campus is just down from where I live and there were lots of strikers outside there yesterday. I saw many wearing new COSATU kit, I might add, and of course the MTN service has had a lot of complaints lately; many callers have called us angry and said they are going to port to other service providers. And in the middle of it all, we have the newly appointed CEO of MTN Mteto Nyati and he joins us . . . Mteto . . . how are you feeling? Gosh you've got a tough job ahead.

MN: – *laughs* – Hey, John, we are all different. Some of us enjoy different kinds of work.

JR: Yeah?

MN: My background is in engineering and what we do as engineers is to address problems.

JR: All right, so you're enthusiastic – are you confident?

MN: Extremely confident. You know, you need to make an assessment of your situation and when I look at the challenges we are facing as a business, most of those challenges are really people-related challenges. And it's quite easy – well never easy – but if it's about engaging people, we can always find solutions.

JR: What are the problems? You came from Microsoft and Aki [Tech journalist Aki Anastasiou] spoke very highly of you. You joined last year so you know what's going on. What are the main problems? This union problem, for example: how long is that going to take because those guys are now part of the furniture on 14th Avenue?

MN: John, on my first day when I was appointed, my first meeting with my team, the first item on my agenda was exactly that – the strike. And out of that we set up a plan to make sure that we end this strike by the end of this week and, in my discussions yesterday with the people who are driving this for me, I have no doubt that we will achieve our objective.

JR: So the strike will be over by the end of the week?

MN: That is our plan and all indications are that we will achieve our objective.

JR: That could cost you a lot of money, couldn't it? To end the strike? Isn't a lot of it about people wanting to be permanent?

MN: If you look at what has happened now – our people, the members of the unions, are suffering, this is a no-work no-pay situation, so as this thing drags out families are suffering and we in turn are facing problems not delivering what we have promised our customers . . . We both want to end the strike. That is what we have set out to do.

The veteran talk-show host wished me luck, sounding doubtful that a two-month-long strike would end by the weekend, two days from then.

But the labour union was ready.

CWU general secretary Aubrey Tshabalala said in a press statement: ' . . . MTN has had a hostile relationship with labour, that arrogance became intense under Farroukh . . . with Nyati leading the negotiations to end the strike, it was clear he knew what he was doing and listened to us.'

Themba and Alpheus, excited at being chosen to resolve the impasse, formalised the agreement with the CWU. Themba seemed grateful for leadership of any kind. Unlike the group chief of HR and corporate affairs Paul Norman who, as I signed my new contract in his office, had said: 'Dead Man Walking . . .'

'What?'

'Dead Man Walking.'

It was, I thought, a strange 'congratulations' from a human capital head. We learn every day. According to him I was going to fail, no matter what.

It had been a futile and damaging period. Striking workers had gone without pay for two months, only to accept the original offer. MTN shares had lost ground as the strike weighed heavily on the stock. Clients were reviewing their contracts. There were no winners.

My first week on the job had been a long one. Finally I could remove my arbitrator's hat and get down to the business of being the CEO of a company that was bleeding customers.

There was plenty of advice from market commentators, who thought I faced an unenviable task. For example, Ovum analyst

Richard Hurst commented: 'It will be interesting to see how he deals with SA's competitive telecoms environment and how he will counter the ongoing consolidation and new entrants into this space. Dobek Pater, telecoms analyst with Africa Analysis, advised: 'He should be focusing on developing the enterprise side of MTN Business and looking to establish content partnership with other players . . . MTN SA needs to become a content provider, which is a key component if it is to be more than just a transmission network.' And ICT commentator Adrian Schofield said: 'The new CEO will need to be nimble and will need to bring a new vision and culture to MTN SA to revitalise it.'

eMpTyN

*As we look ahead into the future, leaders will be those who
serve others, actively listen, and daily empower.*
— *Farshad Asl, Iranian entrepreneur*

My daughter and I entered 2016 with end goals in
mind. Anda set her sights on eight matric As; I had to steer
MTN's return to a customer-centric, profitable entity. Three years
of declining revenue, appalling service, poor network coverage
and slow speeds had the comms giant on the ropes.

Cartoonists dubbed it eMpTyN; consumer websites were lit-
tered with complaints and investors had long lost patience with
its poor performance.

In 2015, a few weeks into my new job, a StanLib manager I
was meeting with had tossed the first-half financial results at
me, completely fed up with being associated with a company
consistently rated the country's worst cellphone service provider.
It sounded as if he'd been relaying this message for too long
without being heard. The sentiments from MTN's other investors were similar.

One positive that came out of my interaction with these investors was connecting with my son, Zukisa. After completing his
Bachelor of Business Science degree at the University of Cape

Town, he had joined the investment team of an asset management firm in Cape Town. While meeting with this firm, one of the portfolio managers told me Zukisa had had the foresight to tell him we were related, so that there was no possible conflict of interest. I thought what he did showed integrity, more so as he was not using my surname. It may not sound like a big deal, but when you have been an absent father, any improvement in the relationship with your offspring, or signs that something may have rubbed off, is a blessing.

But the signs at MTN remained worrying. Three months into my CEO role, President and Group CEO Sifiso Dabengwa resigned after MTN was fined for failing to meet a deadline to disconnect five million unregistered SIM cards. The fine of $5 billion was equivalent to two years of MTN's Nigerian profits. More than $10 billion was wiped off MTN's market value. Sifiso had to take the fall. He announced his resignation to the group executive committee. We were shocked.

MTN Nigeria and others in the industry were frequently fined in Nigeria for non-compliance issues, usually small amounts, which went with the territory. But for some reason in 2015, the Nigerian Communications Commission came up with this $5-billion fine that was completely over the top and restricted to MTN only. It caused a flurry, with other telecommunications companies rushing to avoid the same treatment and hastily disconnecting unregistered users and fraudulent-looking mobile money accounts.

On 9 November 2015, a report in *Biznews*, under the headline 'Axe swings – CEO Dabengwa quits after R60bn wiped off MTN's market value', read:

Cape Town – The embattled MTN announced on Monday that its CEO Sifiso Dabengwa has resigned. MTN, which has been in the spotlight after Nigeria slapped it with a massive \$5.2bn (R71bn) fine for not registering SIM-card holders, announced that Dabengwa has resigned with immediate effect and that Phuthuma Nhleko has been appointed as executive chairperson in a temporary capacity.

'Due to the most unfortunate prevailing circumstances occurring at MTN Nigeria, I, in the interest of the Company and its shareholders, have tendered my resignation with immediate effect,' Dabengwa said in a statement.

Phuthuma Nhleko immediately scheduled one-on-one meetings with group exco members. Mine was the last meeting for the day, set for 7 pm. I'd never met Phuthuma, but I considered him a role model. People who knew him had told me that we shared some traits – he was said to be an introvert, a strategic thinker and not keen on small talk.

I couldn't wait to meet him, so was disappointed when he postponed. When we met two days later, he shared with me how he planned to re-introduce the organisational structure that had catapulted MTN to global success. He didn't ask me for input, but I committed myself to accelerating MTN SA to contribute towards the group's revenue and profit growth.

I set up an emergency strategy session. Usually strat sessions are held with executive committee members only, but I needed to get an unfiltered message across and so invited more than 80 managers from all levels. The facilitators I had chosen for the session protested that they had never dealt with so many people.

I told them there was always a first time and that they could walk away if they didn't want the business. This got their attention and our focus quickly shifted onto how to get the desired results. We agreed to use the 'burning platform' approach – something that Nokia CEO Stephen Elop had perfected. In order to adopt a radical strategy change, you need to convey that it's urgent and painful, like standing on a burning platform in the middle of the sea.

The Net Promoter Score, which gauges customer loyalty, showed us trailing behind Vodacom by fifteen points, which was huge. When you lose ground in the mobile space – as we had done – it's hard to claw back. We had to return the business to growth by transforming customer experience and engaging with employees. The fact that professional people had felt compelled to join a union spoke volumes about their working environment. It couldn't be blamed on external influences – it was MTN born and bred – as was customer dissatisfaction.

As a management team we had to understand our current reality and how we had contributed to the problems we faced. It was a big departure from a defensive culture. The strategy session was uncomfortable for the leadership team. We looked at ourselves in the mirror and didn't like what we saw. And we had proof – numbers don't lie. We had plenty of data pointing to us as the source of our problems.

One of the cartoons I showed staff in a PowerPoint presentation was of a bunch of protestors – in reference to the strike – but the picketers were clients, demanding that their disappearing data be returned.

That wasn't all customers were unhappy about. On social media and consumer sites, they didn't hold back about MTN's seeming inability to communicate, or provide a competitive service:

> – No surprise here consumers!!! To date I have not received a single word from MTN . . . in the interim I have cancelled another contract with them. only 2 more to go then I, a customer of 15 years, will be rid of them!!

> – MTN does not tell you anything . . . on how to cancel, except phoning that ridiculous 808. It might be a free call from an MTN no. but my time holding on is not free, they never answer and the call just gets cut . . .

> – MTN has been debiting my account without permission from March 2015 . . .

> – I have written to mtncustomercare 5x without response! Shocking disregard for your customers . . .

> – Why can't you just send the invoices via email? Your portal is useless when I need to file tax returns . . .

We had to address poor service across our customer channels – call centres, MTN stores, websites, social media and most importantly, the network. Our customer experience was the worst in the industry, instead of a source of competitive advantage. We simply didn't have the right tools to connect with our subscribers and were forever apologising for network downtime and connectivity issues. If customers communicated online, or via social media, there was often no one at the other end to sort out their issues. The call centres were ineffectual.

We came back with a simple strategy to return to growth by transforming customer experience and overhauling employee engagement. In implementing the strategy, I had to assess the suitability of those who had to execute it.

Customer service is a job that has evolved from a soft focus to a core strategic one, requiring an analytical mind, as well as business and process improvement skills. The role involves finding new customers, retaining existing ones and enhancing their experience. This wasn't happening.

I put the leadership team into three mental buckets. The first bucket had to be removed from their positions immediately; the second had to be monitored over twelve months. The third group had the necessary capabilities to execute the new strategy.

Once I had made up my mind on where each of the leaders belonged, I discussed the restructuring plan with Phuthuma and Paul Norman, group chief of HR. I'd learned at IBM and Microsoft that a good plan can be undermined by connected individuals. In my experience, there are always white employees who will try to scupper restructuring efforts being implemented by a black leader. Typically, they'll send emails to senior leaders of the company, painting a picture of chaos, incompetence and reverse discrimination. During my time at Microsoft, many such emails containing complaints about me were sent by my colleagues to leaders such as Steve Ballmer, Kevin Turner, Ali Faramawy and Jean-Philippe Courtois. The tone of the messages was always the same: there is a darkie here running wild. He has no clue what he is doing. Please intervene before your South African subsidiary goes under. Because I had involved key stakeholders who trusted me before executing restructuring plans, these emails always found their way back to me. Not once did I confront the writers. I knew something about them that they did not – always an advantage.

Phuthuma and Paul bought into my plan and we began the painful execution period. None of us wakes up in the morning looking forward to firing someone, but I had to lead from the front. Turning around MTN SA was a job that needed to be done.

I prioritised changes to the information technology, network and customer experience roles and reached out to executive search agencies. After a recruitment process, we employed Ideshini Naidoo from the banking sector. She had been chief information officer at FNB and had a master's degree in strategic IT management.

I said in a statement: 'Naidoo's appointment gives expression to our ongoing quest to improve our customer experience by attracting the right talent and tapping into best practice from other sectors of the economy.'

But our wounded customers were sceptical of anything we promised and continued venting:

> – All customer queries must be sorted out in 24 hours, Nyati said. Yeah right. My last support email took 20 days to get a response.

> – He makes it sound like he can do this overnight. Who is willing to bet a year from now no change has taken place in market share and he has moved on? Just saying.

– Their unethical underhanded behaviour continues. They started to erect a cell tower right in our street without following the proper procedures.

Residents of suburbs where 4G masts had been erected and approved by city councils were having conniptions. Apart from people saying the masts were 'ugly', some believed they caused health problems. I was sceptical about the unproven health hazard, but agreed that in many cases proper protocol had not been followed. Sometimes we'd simply taken the city's lead on where to put masts. There had been an outcry in Lonehill about a mast that we had actually, for once, consulted the residents' association about. I went to meet a delegation of residents at the Indaba Hotel in Fourways. It turned out that their real grievance was against their residents' association, which had ignored their questions and objections and apparently even torn down their protest posters. It was a difficult one: our customers complained about the bad network but didn't want unsightly boosters in their backyards.

Apart from our poor customer relations, our information technology systems were archaic. We needed top talent to introduce cutting-edge technology to enhance customer interaction – people with proven track records in solving complex problems. Again, I thought the best candidates were in the banking sector. At the turn of the millennium, banking systems had been dreadful, but had successfully transitioned to a digital world.

After a considerable search, we appointed Benjamin Marais as chief information officer (CIO). He'd been at Discovery, in charge of Vitality and card systems and before that at eBucks, where he'd played a role in bringing PayPal to South Africa. He was a qualified electrical and electronics engineer, and had worked in Africa, the UK and the Middle East. I was pleased to have found him, but not everyone approved. At one of the quarterly town-hall meetings I introduced to keep staff updated – a first for MTN South Africa – I was asked why, as a black CEO, I had appointed a white CIO. It was an interesting and bold question. I also saw it as a 'team coaching' moment.

The previous CIO, who I had chosen to replace, had been white. In my brief to search agencies I had asked that candidates should be as inclusive as possible. Of the fifteen they'd come up with, including all races and genders, the best applicant happened to be Benjamin, a white man. It wouldn't have sat well with me to take the second, or third best. If MTN was a company that embraced diversity, it had to do that on all levels. I explained this to staff. It was not the answer they wanted to hear, but it was an answer they needed to hear. It was the truth. I needed to set the right tone from the top. The best person for the job couldn't suddenly be the wrong colour. Transformation was a broad process and shouldn't be measured by one or two appointments.

We approached our board to increase our capital expenditure for the year. Twelve billion rand was approved for new infrastructure and we set about transforming our voice and data networks.

We had a two-day joint planning meeting with Huawei, which brought network experts from China. The code name for our network leadership project was 'Catapult'. Vodacom was in our crosshairs. At the end of the planning meeting, in line with Chinese tradition, Huawei offered us gifts, one of which was a painting about half a million rand. In addition, each of our executive committee members was given a high-end Huawei smartphone device.

I stood there looking at the painting, which was of Robben Island, while everybody looked at me, waiting for my response. Huawei was going to be a critical partner in our quest to regain network leadership in South Africa. But my corporate governance training did not allow me to accept these gifts. I explained to the Huawei delegation that MTN planned to make huge investments in its network over the next 24 months. What we did not want down the line was to be accused of having been unduly influenced. I also asked my executive committee members to return their top-of-the-range smartphones. I knew this was not a popular decision.

In July 2016 I had to defend another of my appointments. To outperform Vodacom, MTN needed to double its LTE coverage and roll out new sites, particularly in cities and high-density areas such as malls, freeways and national roads. This process needed the guidance of a world-class chief technology officer, someone who could lead a cross-functional project team. I needed someone with a proven track record of transitioning telecommunication companies from voice to data networks. Developed countries were three to five years ahead of South Africa in this regard.

I knew we wouldn't find the right candidate in South Africa. The previous incumbent had gone to work for Vodafone in the Netherlands. We cast our eyes abroad. One of the leading candidates recommended by the executive search firm was Babak Fouladi, who had been with Vodafone in Romania and Spain.

Before that, he'd been vice president for multimedia and system integration at Ericsson in Russia. I interviewed him at length over the phone and was candid about our problems. If I ended up selecting him, I didn't want him to find out how bad things were only once he'd made the move. Before appointing him, I also wanted to know how he thought our broken systems could be fixed, and be sure that he had the necessary technical skills to achieve desired outcomes. Babak had all the answers and could see the big picture. He would later prove his worth when he was appointed chief technology and information officer for the MTN Group.

To fill his shoes as chief technology officer, I appointed Giovanni Chiarelli, an Italian. Giovanni did miracles with limited spectrum, managing to position MTN as the best network in South Africa in just eighteen months. He and his team took away from Vodacom its only source of competitive advantage.

As I'd told the team at the strategy session, we had to believe it in order to see it. Believing is seeing.

On the HR side, I replaced Themba Nyathi, who chose to focus on his booming side business, with Nhlanhla Qwabe from Aspen Pharmacare. He had experience of dealing with unions and knew they had to be regarded as partners and be properly managed. MTN had viewed them as disruptive enemies. I also created a new role of chief digital officer, appointing Maxwell Nonge, previously of OpenView, to this position. It was a strategic role to move MTN into the new digital world and Maxwell hit the ground running.

Larry Annetts, who had been MTN's chief marketing officer in Nigeria and in Iran, had become chief consumer officer and was clearly the right person for the job, being action-orientated with the ability to break mammoth tasks into chunks that could systematically be dealt with. In Nigeria, the pre-paid market was MTN's bread and butter – we had to try to do the same locally. Larry understood what competitors were doing and was able to come up with value propositions that attracted customers, who, in the pre-paid space, were not loyal. They shopped around for the best deal, be it for more data or cheaper handsets.

To increase revenue we needed to poach subscribers from Telkom or Cell C, which didn't have a national network and roamed on Vodacom. I began engaging with Cell C's chief executive Jose dos Santos to entice him to change to MTN in a network sharing deal. We could offer them 3G and 4G connectivity in smaller cities and rural areas, where Cell C didn't have network and where MTN had extra capacity. We laid the groundwork and this multibillion-rand deal eventually came to fruition in 2018.

In an environment with a growing appetite for data, a new mobile data-only network called Rain had been launched. It was the brainchild of former FNB CEO Michael Jordaan and FirstRand's Paul Harris. They had recently acquired Wireless Business Solutions, which came with high value spectrum. Their intention was to operate only in urban areas and to provide affordable data that never expired. As they needed to partner with an existing mobile network, they approached MTN. To work out the finer details of pricing, I handed the proposal over to MTN SA's chief financial officer, which in hindsight was a mistake. After a month, Rain said they were making no progress and moved on. I was disappointed. It was a critical project that could've changed the structure of the market. I kicked myself for not having led the discussions myself. Instead Rain signed a partnership agreement with Vodacom. It was a big loss for MTN and taught me to follow my instincts. I made a mental note to monitor Sandile and observed on occasions that he and I weren't on the same page. I found him to be deliberately obstructionist. He would feign agreement in meetings, but his subsequent actions demonstrated the opposite. It was a new one on me and I couldn't work out his motives. When the BMF invited me to share with them some insights on leadership, I told them that black CEOs must never assume that they have the support of their black colleagues, which seemed to surprise them. I usually start from the premise that I have no support from any grouping. I then work hard to build a guiding coalition for change.

There were, however, other successful deals, such as one with MultiChoice – to acquire its fibre-to-the-home (FTTH) subsidiary, Smart Village. It accelerated our fibre network strategy and enabled us to chase a new source of revenue in gated estates, business parks and shopping malls. These were high-value customers, so it was worth the R220 million we paid for it.

On 28 September 2015, *IT Web* reported:

> The mobile operator [MTN] has been making aggressive moves in the FTTH space of late. This month, it revealed it is investing around R1,2 billion to upgrade its network in KwaZulu-Natal, starting with FTTH deployment in Durban's La Lucia suburb.
>
> 'The acquisition of Smart Village provides MTN with the opportunity to cement its market leadership in the FTTH space

and to make inroads in the enterprise sector,' says Mteto Nyati, CEO of MTN South Africa.

Things were looking up: for the first time we had gained pre-paid customers, which meant we were starting to attract subscribers from our competitors. From being fifteen points behind Vodacom in 2015, we were now, a year later, only three points shy on the Net Promoter Score. I could look our investors in the eye again.

*

In June 2016 Vodafone's Rob Shuter was appointed president and group CEO of a company facing what was described as the biggest challenge of its 22-year history.

London's *Financial Times* reported that MTN's results 'highlighted the scale of the challenge facing incoming chief executive Rob Shuter . . . tasked with moving MTN on from a dispute with Nigeria's regulator over alleged failure to switch off unregistered users.'

Although what had happened in Nigeria had nothing to do with MTN's South African operation, negative sentiment doesn't help a struggling brand. The unethical label had stuck, no matter how hard we worked.

I am good at picking up signals, even if they are faint. I consider this one of my strengths. And because I spend a lot of time listening to staff, I feel I have valid opinions. But at MTN I was rarely asked for input, which concerned me.

I decided there and then to open myself up to opportunities outside of the MTN Group. When I shared this decision with Zoleka, she was over the moon. I found this odd, as in the past she had always argued for the status quo.

I first met Mteto while doing my MBA in the early '90s at Wits Business School. I was studying full time, he was part time, but we did some elective subjects together in my second year. Like me, he doesn't give too much of himself away. We didn't engage a lot, but I would listen when he shared something because he considers things thoroughly before opening his mouth. It's a valuable quality.

Our paths crossed again years later when I was at MTN. He was looking for local business for IBM and at MTN we were going through a phase of improving our IT capability. In a capital-intensive technology-based business you need sophisticated IT solutions and Mteto and his team helped us work out how to implement them.

After that I followed his career at a distance and, when I was MTN Group CEO, I tried to recruit him. I thought that his academic background and experience with IBM and Microsoft would place him well to help us advance our technology. We were at that stage too dependent on technology suppliers for solutions, rather than determining direction, which hampered our competitive capability. We needed someone who could see things differently and deliver results.

In typical Mteto fashion, his response was measured. He took his time then told me he had no reason to leave Microsoft and that he knew little about mobile business. Why did I want him?

Apart from his IT background, I was looking for someone who had the leadership potential to head MTN sometime in the future. You need to surround yourself with quality leaders dispersed throughout the business who can effectively execute strategies and priorities. It's obviously a risk bringing in someone with limited industry experience at senior level. Just walking into an exco meeting is daunting – what's the first question you're going to ask when you enter an organisation you have little history about? But I thought he would fit in with the culture of the organisation so I persisted and in late 2014 he joined us as head of business – group chief enterprise officer. It was a job in which he had to develop and grow business for us. And grow into a future CEO. Within an organisation you always need a handful of people who can be groomed to take over the top job. This happened sooner than we all thought when Faroukh left in the midst of the strike. It was a nasty time and I think Mteto did a good job under the circumstances. We threw him into the deep end.

I don't remember any particular objections from the board to his appointment. As president of a company you spend most of your time trying to win over your board. That's what they are there for, to challenge and question.

When I left MTN in December 2015 after the Nigerian regulatory fine, Mteto seemed to be coping. I was surprised when he approached me a year or so later and told me he had decided to go to Altron. It clearly wasn't a knee-jerk reaction because that's not the kind of person he is. As I've said, he thinks things through. Once he'd explained his reasoning to me, I realised that it was a challenge he would relish.

I think he's done well in the year or so he's been there. The share price is looking good and that's how I judge things from my perch on the outside.

– Sifiso Dabengwa is a director with Sigma Capital

Chapter 10
Reboot

We all make choices, but in the end our choices make us.
– Ken Levine

Some aspects of my boyhood in Tabase have remained with me. I still wake before dawn, not to do the milk run but to reflect on the day ahead. I catch up with overnight developments via my tablet, quietly, so as not to wake Zoleka, who is a light sleeper.

I love quotes and often start my day by tweeting something I find inspirational. At first I did it for fun, then people began expecting them.

One morning I tweeted: *It is not enough to stare at the steps. You must step up the stairs. Tiptoe if you must, but take that step.*

In hindsight, I realise I was coaching myself.

When I was at MTN I was always the first at work because I would leave home soon after 6 am to beat the traffic. The headquarters of MTN South Africa is in Fairland; it's a state-of-the-art building powered by a methane gas tri-generation plant, piped over 800 km from Sasol's Mozambique gas fields.

I had a big fancy office, although I'd have preferred a space that afforded more interaction with employees. Closed-off offices don't encourage collaboration. I thought to myself then that if I ever had a hand in office planning, I would include staff in the design of the workspace. And have a shared canteen – something I enjoyed at Microsoft – where colleagues could connect. MTN SA leadership seemed to spend more time in internal meetings than engaging with staff and customers. I had to ask employees not to call me 'sir'. I wished it were in my power to change this corporate culture, but big ships are generally hard to turn around.

In May 2016, I was approached by executive search agency Odgers Berndtson. Headhunter Nisha Pillay couldn't tell me which company she was representing until I'd signed a non-disclosure agreement. On my side, too, I had to keep things under wraps. Every time my phone rang I would answer it surreptitiously in case it was Nisha. I didn't want Shenaaz, my executive assistant, to hear me talking about another job. She'd moved from Microsoft to join me at MTN and had played a huge role in the professional running of my office. She was an integral part of the new team I'd assembled to get MTN to a customer- and employee-centric place.

I later met Nisha and a colleague, Modise Makhene, at Tashas Café in Nicolway shopping centre, Bryanston. Modise and I knew each other from Tastic Rice Corporation days and it suddenly dawned on me that he had been behind this approach. I trusted him though.

They disclosed that the Altron group, managed by the Venter family, was seeking a CEO from outside the laager. My interest was piqued because I knew the company well, having done a due diligence when MTN was thinking of buying it. With an annual turnover of R18 billion, it was small in comparison to MTN South Africa, but once manufacturing assets had been offloaded, there would be exciting prospects of transforming it into an ICT company that positively contributed to society.

But the group wasn't doing well. Altron had just delivered the biggest loss in its history. It had also suspended the payment of dividends. This did not please investors.

A number of Altron's manufacturing assets had made business sense during South Africa's isolation in the '80s, but after the lifting of sanctions and the transition to a democratic state, local operations had to compete with global players. What mattered were product quality, affordability and reliability of supply. In the early '90s, I had helped transform Nampak into a world-class manufacturing company through clever use of Japanese manufacturing techniques. On Nampak's side was volume – they had economies of scale. Altron was manufacturing for only a few customers such as Eskom, Telkom and MultiChoice, which made it difficult to sell these assets.

I met with Robbie Venter and his human capital director Johan Klein, and later with lead independent director Mike Leeming, from whom I learned more about the structure of the board. I connected with Mike on different levels. The Venters held 17,8 per cent of the economic rights, including treasury shares, and exercised 57 per cent of voting rights in Altron. It meant that the family's voting power was greater than its shareholding, which didn't make sense. I couldn't accept a job in a company where the family could overrule the board.

The talks stretched over many months, by which time the candidates for the CEO position had been reduced to three. Then in October 2016, Altron secured an equity partner, Value Capital Partners (VCP), an activist investment company that was unfamiliar to me.

The process began afresh as VCP directors Antony Ball and Sam Sithole – former CEO and CFO, respectively, of private equity firm Brait – needed to interview the candidates. They had bought fifteen per cent of Altron – worth R400 million – and needed to be absolutely sure of who was taking over as CEO. Mike kept me abreast of the board restructuring and debt refinancing; these candid discussions sustained my interest in developments at Altron. I would sneak off from work for yet more meetings with the directors and their advisor, former Dimension Data CEO Brett Dawson. In mid-December 2016 I had a final interview with the board's nomination committee, chaired by Penuell Maduna. The committee consulted people I'd worked with – Mark Harris, Ali Faramawy, Brett Goschen and Sifiso Dabengwa – in what seemed like a very thorough process.

*

That December, Zoleka, Anda and I set off for an overseas holiday to Israel, Turkey and the UK. With all the stop-start travelling, I had plenty of time to think about the Altron offer. My short-term goals at MTN were in sight and soon there would be no reason to stay. I daydreamed about how I would be able to use Altron to build a company with a social conscience. This took me back to the Yale World Fellows Program where I had committed to being a leader with a heart. It was also an opportunity to save an iconic South African company and transform it into a global ICT powerhouse. I wanted in.

I looked around me at Israel and saw a country forged from self-belief and a clear vision of its place in the world. Spending Christmas time in the Holy Land of Jesus' birth was spiritual for me. Walking the streets of Jerusalem, visiting the places he preached and healed – the Temple, the Last Supper room – were reminders that he was of flesh and blood with a simple message that could be emulated without having to make a self-congratulatory noise about it.

In England, I visited one of my half-sisters, Mary Nyati, a specialist nurse. She had adapted and, like many who have made the choice to leave their homelands, was keen to justify her self-imposed exile. Privately, I thought it couldn't be easy trying to connect in a country that did not open its arms to you: the Brexit referendum had just happened, and there was xenophobia in the air.

Anda got her eight As and we spent New Year in Turkey, where Zoleka was in her element, having been there before on clothes-buying trips for her business.

Turks have positioned themselves to provide value for money. Top shops in Sandton get their clothing made in Turkey. You can be measured for a suit one day and collect it the next. There had been a wave of terror attacks the year before, blamed on ISIL (Islamic State) and Kurdish resistance groups, so tourism was down and there were bargains everywhere. Zoleka is good at haggling and always negotiates down to the wire. Anda is learning quickly. I don't have the patience for it, but I indulge them. They balance me.

Before I'd left on vacation, I'd been making plans with Professor Njabulo Ndebele and Kusile Mtunzi-Hairwadzi to fundamentally transform the MTN Foundation. Prof. Ndebele was the chairman of the Foundation, Kusile the GM, and they and other trustees seemed excited that I was interested in their work, which partnered with public and private organisations to execute sustainable corporate social investment projects. I wanted to align the foundation with our core business. Now, sitting in Istanbul, I felt guilty. I decided to call the Prof. and inform him of my exit plan. He was happy for me, but said he selfishly hoped things would turn out differently.

A snowstorm in Istanbul delayed our departure. I arrived back in Joburg with my mind made up about my direction – and went straight into the 2017 MTN South Africa Kick Off event. I had introduced this annual event to share business priorities for the year with 3 000 of our employees. We also used it to recognise employees who had performed well. It was also a great platform for group leaders to deliver key messages to MTN SA staff. I was surprised that group executives didn't fall over each other to grab the opportunity to present to this audience. Leadership is more than a position. You must influence, motivate, engage and share priorities with your staff. But our leaders seemed to have trouble standing up and sharing, even when you created a platform for them.

It was a two-day session and there was time for good-natured, self-deprecating humour. Whenever I have the chance, I try to get comedians – such as Mpho 'Popps' Modikoane, Nik Rabinowitz or Chester Missing – to come and poke fun at the serious side of corporate life and at 'important' leaders.

I was in the final stages of negotiating with Altron, and throughout the Kick Off I felt conflicted and hypocritical, knowing I was planning my departure. I felt as if I'd painted a vision for staff and with the canvas only partially filled I was packing my brushes. I felt particularly bad about abandoning my new team, including Shenaaz. At a loss about how to tell her, I worried about it for weeks, even discussing it with Zoleka. Then fortuitously, her engineer husband landed a job in Canada and she resigned. She was distraught; I was relieved.

In late February 2017 – the end of the 2016 financial year – I announced that MTN had taken network leadership position in all major cities, bar Joburg. We were taking the fight to number one – Vodacom – intent on unseating it as the best network in South Africa. Here we were, leading in major cities, thanks to Giovanni and his team. The Net Promoter Scores showed us closing in on No. 1. Perfect. Our customers were the ultimate beneficiaries.

The very same day, I told Phuthuma Nhleko, still acting CEO and board chairman, that I was leaving. I had waited for us to announce our full year results to the market. I did not want our engagement with investors to be clouded by my resignation. He looked shocked and asked if it was about money. I assured him it wasn't; I had a great opportunity to rebuild a local company into a global ICT player and that excited me. In our market there aren't many opportunities dressed in overalls and looking like work. I loved the idea.

'Are you going to Vodacom?' he asked.

It was a strange question. There was a three-year restraint clause preventing me from working for a direct competitor. I told him I was going to an ICT company that wasn't in the mobile space. He said I should go away and reconsider.

When we met again, he told me he'd spoken to the main board and reviewed my package.

'And in "X" years' time you can take over from Rob Shuter. He will hand over to a local person then and who better than you?'

Now you tell me, I thought. Not the best way to manage talent. In any case, my decision wasn't about MTN, or Rob's job. It was about me.

'Phuthuma, you know me, I am a reflective person. My decision is well thought through. I've been in talks with Altron for a long time,' I told him.

'What? You'd leave a global company with a foothold in 22 countries for Altron?'

I repeated that my decision was about growth and opportunity.

'Can you at least stay until the end of June?' he asked.

'I can.'

It was a Friday. I had not yet submitted my formal resignation letter, although I had typed it the week before. Over the weekend, I printed it, signed it and put it in an envelope. On the Monday, after our Cape Town investor roadshow, I gave it to Phuthuma.

It felt like I was betraying a cause. I had wanted to be part of MTN for so long and had dreamed of positioning it in the new digital world. Now I was turning my back on it and signing up to join what some regarded as 'white monopoly capital' at its best. But deep down, I knew I was stalking my passion and could find peace. I heard my mom's voice saying: 'You must do what you like, Dlambulo.'

The following day, Tuesday, Phuthuma called me to ask something odd: 'Please ask Altron not to announce your appointment yet.'

According to JSE rules, if you change your CEO you have to inform your shareholders and the market within 24 hours. You can't sit on the information for weeks and months. Phuthuma said he'd like to have discussions with Altron board's newly appointed chairman, Mike Leeming. I arranged the meeting, but it clearly didn't go Phuthuma's way because Leeming told him Altron had to comply with JSE rules. It was agreed that I would work until the end of June. Both parties would make their announcements on Tuesday, 7 March at 5 pm.

The next day, Altron released a press statement, entitled 'Altron appoints new Group Chief Executive':

JSE-listed Allied Electronics Corporation Limited (Altron) today announced the appointment of Mteto Nyati, a respected ICT executive and business leader, as its new Group Chief Executive.

Nyati was previously the Chief Executive Officer for MTN South Africa and brings a wealth of experience to the Group.

Nyati will assume responsibility as Altron Chief Executive no later than 1 July 2017.

According to Mike Leeming, Chairman of the Altron Board, the appointment of Nyati followed a rigorous recruitment process.

'The Altron Board embarked on a global search for a suitable candidate with the necessary global leadership experience and business orientation with a solid track record in the ICT sector. Mteto has in-depth blue chip technology experience having been at IBM for 12 years and six years at Microsoft prior to joining MTN in October 2014. He has extensive experience in both the business-to-business and business-to-consumer markets. We are extremely pleased to have him on board and are confident that he, the board and Robbie (Venter) will work well together during the handover phase,' said Leeming.

But MTN announced that I would be leaving immediately instead of the end of June, as agreed. Their statement, entitled 'Management changes', made it sound as if I'd been pushed. I suspected they were trying to gain the upper hand.

> The MTN Group advises that Mteto Nyati will be stepping down as the CEO of MTN SA with effect from 13 March 2017. The Company would like to thank Mteto for his role at MTN SA. MTN advises that Godfrey Motsa will assume the position of CEO of MTN SA with effect from 13 March 2017.
>
> The Executive Chairman of MTN Group, Phuthuma Nhleko says, 'The appointment of Godfrey hopefully brings to finality seminal management changes that the Group has had to undertake in the last 12 months. I would like to take the opportunity to thank Mteto for his contribution to MTN SA and wish him the best in his future endeavors.'

The media over reacted and some assumed my departure had everything to do with Rob Shuter taking over as MTN group CEO. On 19 March, the *Sunday Times* reported:

> Until last week Nyati was CEO of MTN SA, which he had begun turning around after a disastrous few years. Then, seemingly out of the blue, he announced that he was leaving to become

CEO of ailing electronics company Altron, which he intends restoring to its former glory . . .

Nyati began talks with Altron in July last year, just one month after MTN announced the appointment of Rob Shuter as group CEO . . .

He says there was 'no connection at all'.

He was very reluctant to enter into discussions with Altron because he had only been appointed CEO of MTN SA a year before and had begun an ambitious turnaround strategy. Which, given that the turnaround strategy he initiated is still far from completion – only half way, he says – makes nonsense of his decision to leave MTN. So why didn't he stay?

'At the end of the day I looked at what was right for Mteto. To take something as complex as this and make something big out of it is a unique opportunity I could not pass over.'

Nyati, 51, says he is at an age 'where I need to be thinking seriously about my legacy. Here you have a great South African company that has not been doing well. And to be part of the turnaround . . . creating a business much bigger than it currently is, beyond South Africa, is something that appeals to me a lot . . .

'Black people like me . . . are largely associated with failures. Rightly or wrongly . . . Here I have an opportunity . . . to turn around a traditionally white business . . . this appealed to me because of what it will mean . . . because we as black South Africans need to be continually demonstrating excellence . . .'

Others, such as *Fin24 Tech*, focused on the collapse of the Venter dynasty. On 26 March, an article appeared under the headline 'Mteto to run the rule over Altron's fortunes':

There is an irony of sorts, given the history of South Africa, that a company started by an Afrikaner engineer at the height of apartheid in the mid-1960s will next month have a black man and an outsider at the helm for the first time.

Former MTN SA CEO Mteto Nyati will take over as CEO of ailing Altron from Robbie Venter, son of Bill Venter – who started the company in 1965 – on April 3.

Under the Venter sons, Robbie and Craig, the Altron group has lost its way and this has caused the Venter family to relinquish control, step aside and look for someone else to run the company for the first time in more than 50 years.

The change comes as Altron made losses in four out of the past five years – in 2016, 2015, 2014 and 2013, including a loss of almost R1 billion in 2013 and a record loss of R1,1 billion in 2016.

Venter senior and Robbie will remain on the Altron board as nonexecutive directors.

My last day was Friday, 10 March 2018, and throughout the day MTNers came to my office to say their goodbyes. 'Why are you leaving us, Mr Mteto?' was the refrain. I'd managed to get them to stop calling me 'sir' – now I was 'Mr' Mteto.

One of them, Lance van Wyk, asked if he could pray for me, which he did for more than ten minutes, leading up to my farewell party. When the MC Nhlanhla Qwabe asked me to address employees, I felt overcome with emotion. I managed to get some words out and told them the truth: that the Altron challenge appealed to me. I still believed in MTN, its leaders, and its strategy. The decision was right for me – nothing else.

The day was emotionally draining. I have never hugged so many people in my life. When I hit my bed that evening I slept the sleep of the contented. In my heart I wished MTN the very best. I would always be their supporter.

One of the first things I did in my new job was to buy shares in Altron, at just over R11 each, a far cry from their heyday when the share price had climbed to R50.

I looked forward to helping the company grow.

I was interviewed for the role of executive assistant at Microsoft in March 2009. I was running late but called to inform Mteto. He sounded very stern over the phone, which naturally made me more anxious than I already was. However, my first impression when I met him was that he was calm, talkative . . . still serious, but very clear about his expectations.

The time I supported Mteto at Microsoft is an experience I will NEVER forget. What stood out was his integrity and his focus on doing the right thing for the business and the right thing for people. His approach and leadership in executing these goals were phenomenal. No ambiguity, but decisiveness and discipline with the highest accuracy, fairness, openness, focused on diversity and inclusion. We planned and worked hard consistently. As an EA, and personally, I connected and shared the same values and similar traits, which made it very easy for me to evangelise.

Mteto was always willing to make time to listen to people. The number of one-on-ones with staff would sometimes outweigh his one-on-ones with the Leadership Team (LT). Mteto kept people matters confidential, but for all other business-related issues he would require me to work through company processes to resolve them.

It was important for him to ensure that he and the LT were enabling staff to do their work and get things done.

Mteto would always portray a seriousness, which kept people

at bay. Staff would first check to see if Mteto's shoes were under his desk before they approached mine. When he moved on to MTN, staff would come to my desk (with tears in their eyes) telling me how much they missed the ritual of looking for his shoes.

One of the first and biggest lessons I have learned from Mteto was not to get excited/flustered about someone else's urgency. His approach/solution was always to find a simplistic way to work. I remember once a colleague commented on my wonderful calm nature and how lucky Mteto was to have my support. My response was that it was in fact Mteto who created the calmness in the executive office!

During my first performance review I started off by mentioning what didn't work well. He stopped the conversation and asked me to focus on what worked well first.

We worked hard and played hard too. During one of our annual trips to Microsoft global exchange conferences in the US, my boss showed off some really cool moves on the dance floor. People were so happy to see Mteto having fun too! But usually he tried to keep things professional and chose not to socialise with colleagues after work. When one of the LT members passed away, I saw a vulnerable side when he admitted at the company meeting that he regretted not using the opportunity of forming a friendship when the LT member had reached out to him.

I supported Mteto at MTN from October 2015 to March 2017. I supported him as he worked on changing MTN SA from a hierarchical, paper-based firm to a flat, open and high-performance organisation. The company culture had already changed when he moved to Altron and staff members were sincerely sad to see Mteto leave.

Mteto has had such an impact on me and my family. We would watch his TV interviews together. My children were so intrigued and motivated when listening to his personal journey. Both my husband and I look forward to his daily words of inspiration on LinkedIn or Twitter, especially now being so far away from home and totally out of our comfort zone here in Canada.

I still miss working with my Boss!

– Shenaaz Aliverdi is Executive Assistant to VP Industrial Affairs & Site Head at Sanofi Pasteur in Canada

Chapter 11

Mbazo

Execution – getting the task done, making it happen – is the most unappreciated skill of an effective business leader.
— *Louis V Gerstner Jr,* Who Says Elephants Can't Dance?

My new office is in Parktown, once the domain of the Randlords who controlled industry in Joburg at the turn of the nineteenth century and built their mansions along the ridge. If I close my eyes I can imagine the clip-clop of horse-drawn cars on dusty streets, echoing the affluence of that time. It doesn't intimidate me, but I feel a need for renewal. The colonial ghosts have lingered too long.

Dingulwazi, the man who brings me my morning tea, is a subservient presence, almost crouching when he puts the tray down, and calling me 'sir'. There are many things to change at Altron House, one of them is this master-servant dynamic.

Similarly, Brigit, the executive assistant I've inherited from Robbie Venter, seems on edge. I think she imagines I'm going to get rid of her because she's part of the old order. I'm more interested in her being able to adapt to my way of doing things and to understand what's relevant for operational efficiency. I don't want my diary filled with irrelevant stuff and will cancel appointments if I haven't been consulted about them. While

I do need to create time for people from outside the company, this obviously doesn't apply to everyone. My priorities are informed by strategy and these are revenue growth, improved profitability, transformed customer experience and employee excellence. If someone is selling computer hardware, a relevant manager can handle the meeting. If it's cloud computing, which is taking off dramatically in Africa's major markets, then I'm interested.

I begin meeting with Brigit every day and she tells me what requests have come in. It's soon apparent to her what decisions she can make without having to consult me. She settles down and gets her confidence back and we start working well together.

Four days into the job, on 6 April 2017, Duncan McLeod interviewed me for *Tech Central*:

> DM: I think a lot of people were surprised when you left MTN. You were midway through a transformation process – you hadn't completed what you wanted to do there?
>
> MN: It was not an easy decision. If you look at all the projects I've done, I always complete them. But this Altron thing comes . . . and you look at the scale of it . . . and I could see it taking me eight years, because it's not just about rebuilding Altron . . . but about taking what you have got and scaling it up to various geographies. And this to me was a much more attractive challenge.
>
> DM: For 51 years this business has been controlled by the Venter family . . . they will remain on the board of directors. You must have had discussions with them? I mean, are there concerns that you will have the family breathing down your neck and second-guessing what you do?

MN: The way to do it is to have a board that is not going to be
represented by any one player. On our board of twelve will be
two Venters and we will clearly benefit from their experience,
but at the same time we have board members with deep
understanding of the ICT space because that's where we
are going. We also have on that board the Value Capital Partners who have invested significantly in this business and
they are bringing value from the finance perspective. I'm comfortable with that structure. To have an independent leader
of this business is going to be good for all shareholders.

Robbie Venter had begun the process of selling off manufacturing assets, but there were still too many disparate businesses
bleeding the company dry. I needed to work out whether to ditch
them, or grow them.

DM: . . . you've got a set top box manufacturer, a vehicle tracking
company in Altech Netstar, Bytes Technology which is
more traditional IT services business . . . are there compati-
bilities between these businesses?

MN: Netstar is something we need to be looking at – can we grow
it, can we take it to other geographies? Does it fit well with
an ICT future? If it doesn't, then what is it we need to do? I
don't want to give answers right now . . . my number one
priority is strategy and linked to that, the operating model.
That's what I want in the next 90 days.

Bringing in a new CEO is an opportunity for a company to exam-
ine itself and ask – is this how a head office should look? Because

I had the advantage of knowing Altron so well, I had worked out that we needed to move away from being a point solution company to becoming a total solution provider. Our customers were reducing suppliers and needing to digitally transform their businesses. We had to redesign our operating model and become more flexible to meet these changing customer needs.

I heard in the passages that my nickname, in isiZulu, was 'Mbazo' – The Axe. It took me back to when Sal Faso arrived to turn around IBM SA in the late '90s. We called him 'The Executioner'. Shedding staff makes everyone jittery.

Exco positions such as corporate affairs, a position Robbie had used as a kind of go-between with government, would become redundant. I could do this kind of networking myself – there was no need for a special person. The corporate finance department was also unnecessary in the Altron I envisaged. In the past the company had grown by acquiring companies that were negotiated and priced in-house by supersmart financial types. But, in my assessment, acquisitions of the future had to be more strategic and selective, and developed by the management team. It was the same with the strategy and corporate sales division. Strategy needs to be owned and executed by the senior leadership team, rather than delegated to a particular department. Also on the chopping block was the corporate sales division; it duplicated the role of central sales, creating silos and unnecessary friction.

The number of chief operating officers could be reduced from three to one. The COO is intended to make the CEO's vision a reality and put ideas into operation. I appointed Bytes CEO Andrew Holden as my COO. He had extensive experience in the IT sector and, as the plan was to move Altron from manufacturing to ICT – cloud computing, data analytics and security – he would be integral to supporting our new strategic direction. All our brands needed to be under a single identity – one Altron. By virtue of making strong contributions to profits, some subsidiaries, such as Netstar, had for too long been left to their own devices. They had to return to the mother ship.

In all the turnaround situations I have spearheaded, I have partnered with the human capital and finance executives, regardless of whether I've felt they, as individuals, fitted in with the envisioned new strategy. Only after twelve months have I acted on the requirements of the business with regard to these roles. Altron was no exception.

The restructuring, we worked out, would see 50 per cent of head office positions made redundant and would save R60 million a year.

I gave board chairman Mike Lemming a heads up when the blueprint was complete and we released a high-level strategy document to the other board members, although they couldn't open it – yet. I wanted to avoid any possibility of it being leaked. Not that any of them would, but stranger things have happened.

Family-run companies are vulnerable in times of leadership transition, especially when an outsider comes in to change business fortunes. There is often conflict between the desire to respect tradition and the need to adapt. But the relevance of the company that once built transformers only for Eskom and decoders only for MultiChoice, had faded. It was a dinosaur, big and cumbersome and wrapped up in old-fashioned thinking.

At the board meeting, I felt for Robbie Venter. It must've been painful to hear that employees he had hired, trusted and nurtured were no longer needed. But, as with all of our discussions, he showed maturity. He pointed out risks and we debated how to mitigate these risks. We agreed that the new strategy was the only way – unpleasant, but necessary. The plan was approved, with a request that the layoffs be dignified and humane.

Along with the group executive of human capital, Johan Klein, and our lawyer, Chris Potgieter, we began the unpleasant process. Some of the mutual separation agreements would take weeks to negotiate, others would take months. In the meantime, I had to earn the trust of remaining staff and find out how they wanted their leaner company to look. Johan and I put together a survey. What did Altronians want to change about the company and what didn't they? Staff members were asked to identify our strengths and to be open about our weaknesses. They were the ones closest to the problems. We needed to become a unified body feeding off each other for ideas and solutions.

Invariably, as often happens when given the chance to unleash, company secrets emerged – from sexual harassment to nepotism. What was also confirmed was that Altronians existed in silos, with little cohesion between various divisions and a meagre understanding of how the company fitted into broader society. We agreed that Altron needed to be a microcosm of what South Africa should look like if managed properly – open, honest, collaborative, progressive and passionate. We had to reflect current socio-economic realities and embrace diversity and inclusion.

People such as Dingulwazi, who meekly served me my tea, needed to feel they belonged.

*

In May 2017, one month into the job, I addressed investors at the financial year-end results presentation in Sandton. Not everyone relishes change – particularly when a black man takes over a traditional Afrikaner company, once the darling of the JSE. But various managerial missteps, including rash acquisitions in East Africa, the non-repayment of debt and the inability to keep up with fundamental technological changes had led to a 77 per cent slide in Altron's valuation since 2007. For this year end, revenue was down 26 per cent, coming in at R19,7 billion. Investors were not a happy bunch.

I tried to keep things upbeat, while making it clear that getting rid of loss-making subsidiaries would be integral to recovery:

> Standing here in front of you after one month at the helm, I am hopeful and I see a bright future . . .
>
> The disposal of the remaining non-core assets remains a priority in order to release further capital to strengthen the balance sheet and enable further investment in the core assets . . . the group expects to complete a number of these disposals in the new financial year – with continued focus being placed on . . . Powertech Transformers and Altech Multimedia.

Powertech, once a leading supplier of electronic equipment, had been losing money hand over fist. It had five operating divisions that designed, tested and manufactured transformers, cables and batteries (such as Willard and Sabat) for boats, jet skis and the automotive market. In 2016, in a bid to reduce the overall debt and stem business decline, Robbie announced plans to dispose of Powertech Batteries. It had begun negotiating with Trinitas, a private equity advisor, to sell the division for R300 million. The deal was eventually concluded on my watch in July 2017.

It wasn't the only Altron loser that had to go. Powertech Transformers had enjoyed exclusive business with Eskom since the '80s, after a Swiss company, ABB, had pulled out during sanctions. Altron had filled the gap and manufacturing transformers became a profitable side of the business. In 2008, it signed a contract with Eskom for R1,3 billion. But then came Zuma and the parastatal capture. For the relationship with Powertech Transformers to continue, Eskom hinted to the previous management that Altron needed 'shareholders'. Altron refused, Eskom stopped buying transformers and a profitable subsidiary dried up. In the 2016/17 financial year end Powertech Transformers announced a R50-million earnings loss before interest and tax.

Soon after taking over, I contacted my old Natal university classmate, Edwin Mabelane, head of procurement at Eskom. Old boy networks can be useful.

But not this one.

We discussed over the phone the subject of Eskom renewing its relationship with Altron. His response was unreasonable to the point of being suspicious. He basically wanted us to sell a stake in the company. To whom, I wondered, but didn't press the issue and we ended the conversation amicably.

Months later, Edwin was named as being involved in the scandalous R600-million Trillian deal with the Gupta family, implicated in state capture, along with CFO Anoj Singh and acting head of group capital Prish Govender. In October 2017, *Daily Maverick* reported:

> Draft charges against Singh detail how Singh, Mabelane and Govender allegedly acted together over a period of months in order to ensure Trillian's payday . . . now face disciplinary charges for allegedly misleading the board tender committee, breaching their fiduciary duties, unauthorised and irregular expenditure and financial misconduct.

In January 2018 Eskom announced that five officials facing serious allegations, including Edwin, had resigned.

*

Finding a buyer for Powertech Transformers remained my obsession, as did the sale of Altech UEC, also a revenue-draining carbuncle. Since 2008, Altech UEC had manufactured and supplied decoders exclusively to MultiChoice and in 2014 had launched a product to compete with DSTV, a satellite-based home entertainment product called Altech Node. Not a well-thought-out move: to compete with your own customer, Multi-Choice. It would cost Altron millions.

When the tender for the supply of state-sponsored decoders went up for grabs in 2014, Altech UEC had applied. In order to meet the June 2015 international deadline to switch from analogue to digital terrestrial TV, the government had to subsidise set top boxes (STBs) to decode digital signals for analogue television sets in five million poor households. Altech UEC was among 26 companies that qualified to be awarded the STB tender and the only one with large-scale local manufacturing capabilities. Because of this, several third parties that wanted to be partners in the tender process approached the company. But Altech UEC decided to go it alone. Of the 26 bidders, USAASA, the agency managing the project, selected six for the initial production stage. Altech UEC wasn't one of them.

Nonetheless, it found itself embroiled in a bribery scandal.

In August 2017, the *Sunday Times* reported that one of President Zuma's sons, Mxolisi Saady Zuma, had allegedly tried to broker a bribe with Altech UEC to help secure the contract by influencing Communications Minister Faith Muthambi. According to the paper, a R54-million 'consultancy fee' was discussed.

The money was never paid, said Altron in a statement:

> Although there was correspondence between Altech UEC and . . . third parties, the company took a commercial decision not to enter into agreements with any of these entitles. No monies or fees were paid to any individual or party related to these engagements.

Early one morning in November 2017, the Competition Commission raided Altech UEC's offices, along with those of a dozen other bidders. These 'dawn raids' – a search-and-seizure process permitted under the Competition Act – were intended to gather evidence of 'cartel-like behaviour'.

We appointed an external legal firm, Bowmans, to conduct an independent investigation into the allegations. It accessed emails going back ten years and found that there had been no anticompetitive conduct with regard to tender collusion and price fixing. All rather unnecessary, I thought, as we hadn't won the bid. The Competition Commission probe continued, delaying the disposal of Altech UEC so crucial to turnaround plans.

In the meantime, we were still trying to get rid of Powertech Transformers. Together with Power Matla, a potential BEE partner, we approached SGB-SMIT, Europe's top medium-sized manufacturer of transformers and, after prolonged talks, a deal was struck. SGB-SMIT signed a purchase agreement for R250 million.

IT Web quoted SGB-SMIT CEO Jan Oelscher, saying: 'The investment into Powertech Transformers is a decisive step to extend our global reach and establish a local presence in Southern Africa. With our partner Power Matla, we will strengthen Powertech Transformers as the leading supplier of transformers in the region. We look forward to working with them and continuing our growth story together.'

But then, to my dismay, the deal faltered.

During the 2008 economic meltdown I was working at a restaurant in Parkview, Johannesburg.

There was this regular customer of mine who always lifted my spirits when he came to the restaurant, not necessarily with the way he tipped, but the interaction with him left me in a better place as a human being. I had no idea who this guy was, but I realised that my boss was very jumpy and panicky whenever this man came to dine. When I learnt that this was one of South Africa's most prominent businessmen, I was stunned. In my previous conversations with him, he had not mentioned any of his accomplishments to me. My customer's name was Bill Venter then founder and chairman of the JSE-listed group Altron.

One day Bill called me to the table where he sat with his wife Penny, and he said to her, 'Tell him, darling'. Penny then broke the news to me that they were impressed by my work and they would like to have me work at the Altron Head Office in Parktown, Johannesburg. In January 2009, I joined the Altron group; my immediate task was to look after the top management and guests.

At the age of 30 I enrolled for evening classes to write my matric exams; after work every Monday to Friday I would attend two-hour lessons at Ikaheng Barnato High. I passed matric with two distinctions. Meanwhile, Altron was busy with plans to transform from a wholly owned family business to an indepen-

213

dent one. At Altron, news broke about a new CEO that was coming to 'shake things up'. Mteto Nyati was duly introduced on the 3rd of April 2017. Staff at Head Office feared for their jobs because nobody knew who exactly Mteto was. What leadership style would he adopt? To put Altron back to its former glory Mteto had to do a few unpopular announcements, notably when three top executives were let go. That earned him the nickname Mbazo (the chopping axe). Mr Nyati has a very sharp eye when it comes to people. Early in the morning he will greet you and ask if everything is ok. I must admit my initial take on him was that he is an astute businessperson with no emotion for staff and cares only about the bottom line. He proved me wrong when he showed me that he does not manage people as if they are robots. He wants to understand people's feelings so as to take appropriate decisions. Some leaders love being revered and feared, but all Mteto wants is mutual respect and professionalism in a workplace. He gives me the same amount of respect as he would to a fellow exco member.

With his unique and modern approach, he makes you feel appreciated and valuable no matter what position and status you hold.

– Dingulwazi Makwelo works in Altron IT Support

Chapter 12

Company and Country

If we want a great nation, we have to change it ourselves.
– Cory Booker, US Senator

When I began writing this book, South Africans were trapped in a morass of bad political leadership from which we seemed unable to free ourselves. When we eventually emerged, unsure of whom to trust, it was in the hope that politicians had learned that factional leadership and blind loyalty will fail you, sooner or later. Business is like politics: both need leaders who set themselves apart, but who are able to connect and create an environment in which everyone can thrive. Not just a select few.

I entered 2018 more confident in my country's leadership.

But then something happened that almost scuppered the Powertech deal and made me even more aware of how business mirrors society.

In March, the National Assembly adopted the EFF's motion for parliament's constitutional review committee to investigate expropriation of land without compensation. The Germans, on the cusp of acquiring Powertech Transformers, got cold feet, envisaging a Zimbabwean scenario in South Africa's not-too-distant future, in which multinationals and privately owned land would be taken over. Why invest here if they could put their money elsewhere, in countries where there were opportunities for growth and space for new ideas?

What irritated me was that when SGB-SMIT signed the purchase agreement with Altron in November 2017, South Africa's prospects had been far worse, with the possibility that whoever took over the ANC would continue to serve factional interests. With that threat averted, how could we convince foreigners reacting to headlines and negative sentiment that we were significantly better off with Ramaphosa in charge? Obviously, any persuading from me would reek of self-interest.

I had to find movers and shakers who could make the Germans feel comfortable by providing clarity and policy certainty. I refused to allow perceptions to kill the last hope of selling Powertech Transformers and saving the jobs of 800 employees. We had factories in Pretoria and Cape Town and sales offices in Durban, Cape Town and Nairobi.

I suggested that before making a final decision, SGB-SMIT executives should come to South Africa to properly assess the political climate and investment opportunities.

I managed and thought I would have a few weeks to plan and set up the visit.

To my relief they agreed, but to my dismay said they would arrive in two days. I hadn't even had a chance to speak to anyone influential, let alone arrange the logistics such a visit would require. Securing meetings with government officials and senior executives at short notice is difficult. They are often booked up weeks in advance.

I'm not a panicker, but I came close. I began calling in favours.

It reminded me of when IBM General Manager Johann Weihen had told me to contact him if I ever needed anything: I hadn't acted on his offer until I'd truly needed his help to secure my European posting. Now a R250-million deal was almost on the rocks, so I cast my net far and wide to business acquaintances.

I got hold of Nedbank CEO Mike Brown. Shortly after the appointment of the new Eskom board, the embattled power utility had asked banks for a R20-billion loan. The banks, which included Nedbank, wouldn't have granted the loan if Zuma or one of his cronies had still been in charge, nor without thoroughly assessing future risk scenarios. Mike's input and that of his managing executive for investment banking, Brian Kennedy, would be key in helping to persuade the Germans that Eskom's governance issues were a thing of the past. I also phoned Eskom board chairman Jabu Mabuza. He was flying into Joburg on the Wednesday (two days from then, the day SGB's directors were due to arrive in the country) and was going straight to an Eskom strategy session. However, he agreed to give up his lunch hour to meet the German delegation, as did Lionel October, the DG of Trade and Industry, and Tshediso Matona, who was by then attached to the Presidency. Tshediso had helped us with the Microsoft BEE deal when he was still at the DTI. Bonang Mohale, the CEO of Business Leadership SA, was out of the country, but asked the COO, Busisiwe Mavuso, to make herself available.

Brigit followed up the requests by email and we began planning how to see everyone in different places in such a short space of time.

Lionel was presenting in parliament, but agreed to step out

to do a conference call. He also arranged for us to meet his deputy, Sipho Zikode, in Pretoria. Mike Brown had no gaps during the day, but said he would see us after hours at his Sandton offices.

It was a mad 48 hours of back-to-back meetings, travelling in convoy, to reassure the Germans that, although South Africa's challenges hadn't gone away, new political leadership meant we were more capable of dealing with them.

It worked.

On 26 July 2018, *Tech Central* reported:

> Altron has taken another big step in shedding its legacy industrial assets as the JSE-listed technology group transforms into an ICT-focused business.
>
> It said on Thursday that it has finalised the disposal of its 80% stake in Powertech Transformers to a broad-based black economic empowerment consortium made up of European transformers company SGB-SMIT and the black-owned Power Matla Group in South Africa.
>
> 'The conclusion of the disposal of Powertech Transformers is an achievement for my executive leadership team and me. We will now invest our time on what matters most and apply renewed focus on driving key levers of our strategy which will fast-track our growth,' said Altron CEO Mteto Nyati in a statement.

I tweeted: *Today Altron concluded the sale of Powertech Transformers. We wish our former colleagues the very best for the future.* SGB-SMIT *is so lucky to have them. #KeepShining*

The strong relationship I built with SGB-SMIT CEO Jan

Oelscher saw the deal through. It was a relationship based on trust. Its foundations were honesty and openness. At times I was the lone voice for the deal and if something had gone wrong, my credibility would've been out the window. What kept me going during these difficult internal discussions was the trust and respect Jan and I had for one another.

The headache that was Altech UEC remained. In another era, set top boxes had been viable business, but now they were produced cheaply in China, so the cost structure of producing them locally was way out of line and it made no sense to continue. While we waited to be cleared by the Competition Commission, we began negotiating with one of China's top electronic enterprises, Skyworth Digital, which needed local manufacturing capabilities.

With non-core assets almost disposed of, I could get on with the process of aligning our subsidiaries under one roof, paying back long-suffering investors and making Altron relevant to South Africa. We needed to make money and be impactful.

In the field of public safety, I envisaged a greater role for Netstar: one of Altron's strategic business units and a pioneer of stolen vehicle recovery technology. The crime situation in South Africa has enabled us to become world leaders in anti-theft technology, such as Netstar's Jamming Resist, which can circumvent car thieves by detecting signal interference and sending an emergency message on a different frequency to the one being jammed.

But while its technical capability in the field of telematics and fleet management was impressive, Netstar had been underperforming – mainly because there hadn't been much aggressive engagement with customers, or enough strategic geographical expansion.

We began exploring channels to exploit existing relationships abroad. In 2015, Altron had acquired an Australian company, Pinpoint Communications, which developed hardware and software for vehicle telematics and diagnostics. Fleet management was a highly fragmented market in Australia, so in 2017 we bought out a major competitor, EZY2C, for R163 million. The acquisition would, I announced in a press statement, 'extend our presence into new territories not covered by Pinpoint . . .'

The unit began seeking partnerships in Europe and Asia, companies that could generate income streams and move us beyond vehicle recovery and fleet management. In October 2018, we would sign a joint venture deal with a US-based company, C Ahead Technologies, to offer fleet telematics to India. Only two per cent of India's nearly 200 million cars are 'connected', so the scope is huge. The commercial vehicle telematics market is expected to grow by about 25 per cent per annum – in things like wireless connectivity, navigation and remote diagnostics.

Soon afterwards, during an interview on *CNBC Africa* television network, I told anchor Godfrey Mutizwa why we had decided to go offshore:

> We love SA, we will continue to be here, but with the ups and downs of the economy here, you need a balanced portfolio. So we felt we needed to have operations in Australia and in the UK. Last year, we made an acquisition in the UK, a company called Phoenix Software that has contributed very positively to our results . . . we are also looking to establish Netstar in the

UK, Germany and Malaysia . . . but right now our focus is on fixing our business here in SA.

Fixing business in South Africa meant building capacity. We needed skills, which were in short supply in the fields of data analytics and cloud computing. Before they even leave university, most young data scientists are snapped up by big players such as Google, Microsoft and Amazon, so we either had to build up our own skills, or acquire small companies with those capabilities. By acquiring talent and creating a favourable environment, Altron could become a company where other skilled people want to work.

We began looking locally and identified IT company iSPartners, which had a Microsoft-focused subsidiary called Karabina, as well as Zetta Business Solutions, which provided data advisory services. We had already made a strategic decision to align ourselves with Microsoft in the cloud-computing space – partly because of my past relationship with MS and because it had the technology capacity to move companies to the cloud. Through iSPartners and its bright young data analysts Altron could assist state institutions, as well as businesses, to digitally transform.

But we weren't the only ones sniffing around iSPartners. There were others interested too, even a global player. iSPartners CEO Grant van der Wal and his team were undecided. Should they continue to grow on their own, or align with a bigger company to access significant customers abroad?

I met Grant, together with my group executive of shared services, Collin Govender, and COO Andrew Holden. In the past, these were discussions the corporate finance division would have handled. But because there was no longer such a division at Altron – and because I sensed that the decider wouldn't be about money, but values, culture and vision – I led the crucial discussions.

We spent two hours talking, not about technology, but about the kind of company we were building and how our combined businesses could impact on society. And that, in the end, is what separated us from the rest. The discussions took two months, with a cooling-off period in between. Altron board member Sam Sithole and an investment committee did the due diligence, gave us the go-ahead and talks resumed again. And so, in a deal worth R225 million, Altron Karabina was born.

Grant van der Wal said in a statement:

> This is a key announcement for the South African IT industry, which needs a partner that brings business scale in data analytics and cloud computing . . . with this deal we aim to be that partner . . . relevant to customers and their business requirements, which aligns to Altron's core purpose of providing innovation that matters.

And I told *IT Web*:

> The Fourth Industrial Revolution is here. The digital world is advancing at high speeds and this has an enormous impact on how businesses of the future will operate. To maintain a competitive advantage in a cloud-first and mobile-first world, businesses need to embrace digital transformation using innovative

ways of connecting people, managing data, and streamlining processes to create value for customers. Our solutions will enable our customers to successfully embark on that journey. With 200 employees and the recipient of over 70 local and international industry awards, Karabina is uniquely positioned as a 'Microsoft partner of the future'.

*

Towards the end of September 2018 I, along with 66 other CEOs, was invited to the Union Buildings by the minister in the presidency Dr Nkosazana Dlamini-Zuma for a think tank with economic development minister Ebrahim Patel and Mpumi Mpofu, DG in the Department of Planning Monitoring and Evaluation.

We spent three hours in the East Wing – a collection of CEOs and government's top planners – rekindling a damaged relationship. Under Jacob Zuma's presidency the private sector had found itself a scapegoat for government inadequacies. I didn't like the way that the fault lines of our country had been exploited with talk of radical economic transformation. There is a formula for success and we need to get our heads around the fact that if we constantly harp on about race and the past we will never move forward. In the long term we will destroy what has been built. Companies already in the market need to feel comfortable and unthreatened by talk of nationalisation and white monopoly capital. The sooner we stop revering big talkers and start embracing a culture of education and entrepreneurship, the better.

Take Business Connexion – BCX – founded by twin brothers, Isaac and Benjamin Mophatlane, Sbu Shabalala's Adapt IT and

Xoliswa Kakana's ICT-Works. They didn't say, 'Let's go and break white companies like IBM or Dimension Data in order to make space for us.' They looked at creating something unique that would help them stand out and be competitive. Altron exists as a world-class technology manufacturer because, back in the '60s, its founder did not beg the British for cake crumbs. He set out to find niche sectors and come up with ideas of how to compete. As black entrepreneurs, there is so much we can learn from the likes of Dr Venter.

If you can create a company that can survive in South Africa today, it can survive anywhere. That is radical economic transformation – creating enterprise in new growth areas, not destroying existing enterprise. Let's rather create excellence.

I looked around the room. Former constitutional development minister and skilled negotiator Roelf Meyer was there. The meeting was a result of dialogue between him, Minister Dlamini-Zuma and skilled business leader Johan van Zyl, the first African to be appointed a senior managing officer at Toyota head office in Japan. Meyer and Van Zyl had first met with President Ramaphosa at Tuynhuys, requesting him to clear obstacles preventing economic growth in exchange for getting the private sector to contribute more meaningfully towards the NDP – the National Development Plan – the objectives of which are to eliminate poverty and reduce inequality.

In the discussions at the Union Buildings, we divided ourselves into sectors and each agreed to come up with a five-year plan. I was tasked with co-ordinating the ICT cluster, along with Doug Woolley from Dell and IBM's Hamilton Ratshefola. We had to report back in two months with a plan that would form the basis of sectoral efforts to aid economic growth, protect what was working in business and find creative ways for new players to come in. In turn, government would provide an environment conducive to this, as well as less punitive legislation.

In late January 2019, CEOs met with the president under the Public Private Growth Initiative to present the sector growth plans and highlight growth inhibitors. I presented on behalf of the private sector and spoke about the need to make doing business in South Africa easier and to address policy, legal, regulatory and administrative barriers that frustrate investors. The government delegation received the input well and agreed to address the growth inhibitors with a sense of urgency. Some of our ideas would be fed into President Ramaphosa's second State of the Nation address.

I left the meeting encouraged by the atmosphere of trust. And also because it was tangible stuff, driven by self-interest. Government will help you if, in return, you help it grow an inclusive economy and enhance the capability of the state by working together to solve complex problems. In trying times, with more than six million unemployed and rampant crime, smart people need to engage.

This is Altron's vision anyway. After the announcement of the first financial results under my watch, we briefed our partners, as well as fund managers and bankers gathered at the JSE, about the practical ways our business units could make a difference in areas such as safety and security, healthcare management, skills development and financial inclusion. I'm usually cautious about talking too much about plans before they are a reality, but in this case Altron was already well advanced in developing the technology needed to create smarter and safer cities. As for the other areas, I touched on Altron's provision of broadband infrastructure, stolen vehicle recovery services, fleet management, biometric identification services and workforce management systems. And in the private healthcare system, Altron's provision of the information technology infrastructure that enables medical practitioners to effectively manage their practices and connect them to health funders and pharmacies. We cannot think about being smart – or safe – in this day and age unless there is connectivity. It's an economic and social enabler.

In Gauteng, one of our subsidiaries, Altron Nexus, had rolled out 1 600 km of high-speed fibre optics, connecting community centres, development zones and several hundred schools. In March 2018, we were awarded a contract to provide ICT connectivity to government departments, municipalities, businesses and 1,6 million households in Limpopo. Being Limpopo, it wasn't without controversy and a few months later an article in the *Sunday Independent* described the deal as a 'fiasco'.

> Limpopo's R585 million broadband project hangs in the balance as the consortium of companies appointed to lead it squabbles over money.
>
> The squabble comes after Altech . . . reneged on the initial agreement that would have seen six SMMEs getting 33% of the pie amounting to R192m.

According to the newspaper, the State Information Technology Agency was 'seething' and had 'cautioned against government departments using Altech services and infrastructure'.

If the *Sunday Independent* had bothered to get hold of us we would have told them that our small black businesses partners in Limpopo hadn't been paid because they hadn't done anything yet. The broadband project spanned three years and the build portion of the physical fibre rollout, of which they were part, had yet to commence. We were still in the hardware and software deployment phase and payment by Limpopo Connexion, the provincial ICT development agency, had been for equipment to be ordered and shipped. But we should have communicated better with our SMMEs and they wouldn't have felt the need to go to the press. Lesson learned.

The article had stated that 'attempts to get comment from Altech were not successful'. I sometimes wonder if journalists 'attempts' become rather half-hearted when they feel the response may interfere with their storyline.

I have a good working relationship with the media, having become conscious, while working at Microsoft, of the role journalists can play in helping to sell the future of a company to sceptical investors, shareholders, bank lenders, potential employees and customers. I always make time for media houses, even if it means going into radio or TV studios in the evenings after work. There was much to communicate when I took over at Altron. The public needed to know that this conservative Afrikaner company was no longer a family-run business, but that it was transforming itself into a world-class and inclusive ICT company with global aspirations.

In February 2018, when JJ Tabane interviewed me on *Power FM*, I used the opportunity to promote Altron's new look:

JJ: How many blacks are in your leadership team?

MN: I arrived at Altron 11 months ago and the whole leadership
      team was white.

JJ: You serious? 11 months ago you had a lily-white situation?

MN: And today 50% of that leadership team is black . . . we have
      8 600 employees and 67% of those are black, but largely at
      lower levels.

JJ: Did you have to add blacks to the team? How did you get
      to 50%?

MN: We made some tough decisions and today we are starting
      to reflect South African society at senior level . . . our exco is
      a team of 12 people – and 50% of those people are black . . .
      there were also no women before. Now we have women as
      head of marketing and HR. We need to create a company
      that is diverse. One of the discussions we often have is: do
      we hire people who are different to us?

JJ: So you would rather have people with your vision than to
      give them a carrot and a stick?

MN: We don't need carrots and sticks to incentivise people. We
      need those with a deep understanding of our values – that
      is what guides us. And if we've got people who are not liv-
      ing the values, they may have to work elsewhere.

I enjoyed my chats with JJ and was sorry when he got the boot
from *Power FM*. Journalism needs intelligent people like him. I
get fed up when basic research isn't done and storylines aren't
changed, despite facts changing. Or when they miss the point
completely. In May 2018, when we announced our full year
financial results for 2017, most publications were reporting on
our recovery with headlines such as:

'Altron to resume dividend payments, pursue acquisitions . . .'

'Altron reaping rewards of turnaround strategy . . .'

'Altron eyes next phase of growth following turnaround . . .'

It was a classic good news story. A year before, Altron had been all but written off. Now, for the first time in three years, we could reward our shareholders. Straight after a Q&A session at the JSE, I did interviews with *Moneyweb*, *CapeTalk*, *Radio 2000* and *Business Day*, then flew to Cape Town to brief major shareholders such as Coronation and Sanlam, which had seen their shares plummet to R6 after buying them for double that. Now they were at R14.

On 11 May 2018, I received an unexpected email from Bill Venter:

Dear Mteto,

It behoves me to congratulate you and your executive team, as well as all of our Board members, and in fact, the people of Altron, for your combined fine efforts in producing such excellent year end results for the group and announced in the media today.

The overall recovery of the group, under your careful watch, has been nothing less than amazing and this significant achievement is something to be really proud of.

The 'OneAltron' strategy that you have introduced during the past few months appears to be working extremely well and our repositioning as a strongly competitive ICT company continues to be highly successful.

In fact, considerable progress has been made right across the board and I am highly delighted with the results and what has been achieved since you joined us as Chief Executive Officer a year ago.

My sincere thanks and heartiest congratulations,
Yours sincerely
Dr Bill Venter
Chairman Emeritus

But one particular journalist decided instead to focus on our 'lean head office structure' and reported that 'when factoring in discontinued operations, overall group revenue declined by 10% to almost R17.7 billion'. The year before, when the Public Investment Corporation had reduced its Altron shareholding, for matters to do with the Venter family dissolving their shareholding structure, this same journalist reported this as evidence of a 'lack of confidence . . . that could spill over into other investors . . . who will begin to re-evaluate their positions in Altron . . .'

Either she was ill informed, or she had preconceived ideas about black leadership. I suspected the latter. Her assumption was that a black CEO would mess up. I made a point of asking our marketing team, led by Zipporah Maubane, to 'manage' certain journalists better – particularly those who consistently misrepresented our financial results. As part of our strategy, we offered journalists one-on-one meetings with me to give them an opportunity to ask questions. Most welcomed this and it resulted in articles that had more depth. However, these engagements never addressed the issues we had with specific journalists who, it seemed, chose to misunderstand us. We decided that instead of getting hung up on it we would simply focus on operational excellence and consistently deliver on market expectations. This appears to have silenced the critics.

Communication through the media is key. If we don't provide information, how will ordinary people know that Altron assists money-lending businesses to do client assessment; that our systems connect public healthcare to patients; that Bytes Document Solutions is the world's biggest Xerox distributor and that Bytes UK is the biggest licensing partner of Microsoft products in the UK?

*

In November 2018, for the first time in a long while, I wrote an opinion piece for the *Sunday Times*. I had felt constrained during the Zuma years and, like many, had found it difficult to express an unequivocal position. Now I felt free to convey the importance of leaving positive footprints – of managing assets for future generations and preserving a legacy of values and ethics. And I wasn't referring to business only. Government needed proper vision. My article was entitled 'Everything but vision from Cyril':

> Stewardship is one of the most important responsibilities of leaders. It is a concept that was lost on former president Jacob Zuma. As such, President Cyril Ramaphosa inherited a burning platform, which immediately demanded that he leads his cabinet in the execution of a turnaround strategy for SA Inc. This was the logical course of action for him and remains an unenviable

task for any leader, particularly when turning around the fortunes of a country . . .

Every successful turnaround follows specific steps . . . applicable in any scenario, be it business or government. The first step is to focus on understanding the problem. Ramaphosa was SA's deputy president – he had a prime seat at the table to watch the wrecking ball that was his boss. He understood the mess that had been created.

The second step is to develop and communicate a compelling vision. When he was campaigning to become ANC president, he came up with the 'new deal for SA'. This was seen as the genesis of his post-Zupta vision – the New Dawn . . .

The perceived EFF threat on the land question completely derailed him from crafting a unifying and compelling vision for SA. This is a gaping hole in our country's turnaround strategy. The land question is urgent and requires absolute clarity on its implications for all. Inclusive growth is also important for the success of SA. The president's prioritisation of the divisive land question has sent jitters across SA and the world – his focus on the issue may have silenced some of his critics within the ANC, but he has certainly alienated critical growth partners.

The third step in a turnaround is to establish a few vital goals and pursue them relentlessly. The president has set himself these goals and moved with speed to fix state-owned enterprises, replacing compromised board members with people of integrity. He has appointed four special envoys and an economic advisor whose goal is to raise $100bn in five years. It is a big, hairy, audacious goal . . .

The fourth step is to clean the house at the top. The president had an opportunity to bring fresh blood into his new cabinet, thereby cleaning the house completely. He missed the opportunity – his pick of ministers included questionable politicians but he did well with others, particularly Tito Mboweni . . .

It's urgent that, when in a turnaround, you immediately find ways to stop the bleeding and focus on core activities. I found minister Mboweni's views on SAA and the Reserve Bank interesting – he sees SAA as a resource-hungry yet noncore asset to the recovery of the economy, making it a good candidate for closure. This action may not be popular, but it is what is needed. Minister Mboweni seems to know that the harder thing to do and the right thing to do are usually the same. More of his comrades should bite the bullet and follow suit for the sake of the country.

The fifth step is to inspire and deliver a message of hope. It is important for the president, in words and actions, to shift the country's mood from despair to hope . . . The message of hope is taking hold – at a recent investment conference, local companies pledged R290bn of investment. These early wins will engender hope . . .

As you close on your turnaround, the last step is to create supporting alliances. The president is doing a great job in mobilising business, Cosatu, Sanco and religious organisations behind his New Dawn . . . he needs to continue building a coalition of the committed.

The big threat to Ramaphosa's turnaround strategy is the lack of a unifying and compelling vision. The vision that the president had was derailed by the land issue. We need a new vision; we need all South Africans to put their shoulders to the wheel around the same goal. People will commit if their future is secured. Our constitution states that SA belongs to all who live in it – a good starting point for creating an inclusive and compelling vision.

Cyril Ramaphosa is no stranger to our constitution. He and Roelf Meyer led the process of crafting it. In my mind, the preamble to the constitution captures the essence of the kind of country we are building:

> We, the people of South Africa, Recognise the injustices of our past; Honour those who suffered for justice and freedom in our land; Respect those who have worked to build and develop our country; and Believe that South Africa belongs to all who live in it, united in our diversity. We therefore, through our freely elected representatives, adopt this Constitution as the supreme law of the Republic so as to – Heal the divisions of the past and establish a society based on democratic values, social justice and fundamental human rights; Lay the foundations for a democratic and open society in which government is based on the will of the people and every citizen is equally protected by law; Improve the quality of life of all citizens and free the potential of each person; and Build a united and democratic South Africa able to take its rightful place as a sovereign state in the family of nations. May God protect our people. Nkosi Sikelel'iAfrika. Morena boloka setjhaba sa heso. God seën Suid-Afrika. God bless South Africa. Mudzimu fhatutshedza Afurika. Hosi katekisa Afrika.

The political space is a cacophony these days. Manyi, former BMF president, now talks about decolonisation; the EFF's Julius Malema about land expropriation without compensation; Black First Land First's Andile Mngxitama about murdering white people. Missing are voices of reason calling on South Africans to embrace their constitution. We need leaders who can put forward a case for diversity and inclusion. It is not an easy message.

Our president should be delivering this message every time he speaks.

South Africa's transition to democracy wasn't a miracle. It was thanks to the hard work and conscious effort by Mandela, Mbeki, Tambo, Sisulu and others. If there was ever something they wanted Cyril to do it was to finish the national reconciliation project – even if the challenges seem insurmountable.

Your moment has arrived, Cyril. *Ixesha lakho lifikile Matamela.* Seize it.

From: Anette Klopper du Toit
Sent: Friday, 22 March 2019 4:41 PM
To: Mteto Nyati
Subject: Thank you.

Hi Mteto

I was hoping to chat to you for five minutes at the Kick Off sessions, but everybody wanted a piece of you. I really don't expect you to remember me: I am the lady who almost lost her balance on Sunday night when I received my long service award.

I just wanted to say thank you for being such an amazing leader: a leader who not only shows the way but who also walks the way with his team.

During the awards I really admired the fact that you treated every individual with the same amount of respect. That same smile and kind words. Even when I almost lost my balance, you still told me I did really well. Mteto, you have no idea how much that meant to me. Your encouragement means a lot to me. I admire your leadership and decision-making skills. I hope to continue learning from you and appreciate all your encouragement and support.

Thanks for giving me an opportunity to work with you – for the group. We are grateful to you for directions instead of orders; thankful for giving us a vision instead of targets; proud of you for your inspirational and one-of-a-kind guidance.

Mteto, I have worked for large corporate companies before, but you raised the bar, sir. I admire you for that. You have my commitment and continuous support.

'Leadership is not about titles, positions or flow charts, it is about one life, influencing another.'

Regards,
Anette Klopper du Toit
Manager – Risk Control
NUPAY
A DIVISION OF ALTRON

Chapter 13

Betting on a Darkie

We're here for a reason. I believe a bit of the reason is to throw little torches out to lead people through the dark.

– Whoopi Goldberg

Show me a successful individual and I'll show you someone who had real positive influences in his or her life. I don't care what you do for a living – if you do it well I'm sure there was someone cheering you on, or showing the way. A mentor.

– Denzel Washington

In August 2018 we held a family gathering to remember my mother, fifteen years after her passing. The celebration of her life should have been in Tabase, but vandals had laid the old family house to ruin, so we had the commemoration in Mthatha. Afterwards, a few of us went out to the village.

The vibrancy of my childhood years would be hard to explain to a newcomer to Tabase. As we drove in, along the same dirt road my half-brother and I had traversed on so many early mornings decades before, I saw the communal agricultural land lying unused, the same land that had once fed many families. In a country where there is overnight success, hard work seems to have become uncool. When I looked at Jumba Secondary School, the outdoor gym equipment I'd once donated to the soccer club stood neglected in the long grass. I wondered about the planned 'expropriation of land without compensation'. What has freedom done to our communities? Did the string of promises from our leaders kill individual initiative? It makes me sad.

Embekweni Store, where I learned the ground rules of what I practise today, is forlorn and abandoned. Ntombi Saziwa, the woman who'd looked after my parents and the shop when they were no longer able to, inherited the business and the house, but couldn't cope with the level of criminality. Thugs stole everything from under her nose and what wasn't looted was broken. We moved her to my parents' Mthatha home.

The sense of community I'd felt growing up in Tabase has gone. Poverty and criminality are everywhere. Inside our old home, doors had been kicked in and windows stripped, but the carpeting was still on the floors, the landline telephones still plugged in. Reminders of a bygone age when this was home to twelve of us . . .

My parents' burial site is a kilometre from the old homestead in tranquil surrounds, green hills rolling across the horizon.

Nombeko Annie Nyati
1933–2003

The light that you have been to us and to those
whose lives you have touched will shine forever.
Siyakukhulula, Phumla Ngoxolo Jolakazi.

Michael 'Mike' Mtutuzeli Nyati
1929–2007

Bhele Elikhulu
You've fulfilled your life purpose.
Your legacy will live on through us.

None of us has lost what my parents taught us – respect for others, a sense of purpose and the importance of diversity. Above all, my mother wanted us to be independent beings; my father's priority was that we be educated. Today, two of us are engineers and two are in the medical field. My youngest half-brother, whom my mother put through university, is a lawyer. My three half-sisters are qualified nurses, some working in the UK. My daughter is studying neuroscience in the US; my nephew completed his engineering degree there.

But perhaps if we'd grown up in poverty, with absent parents who did not have the means to provide for us, I may have continued sniffing petrol and glue in Tabase. Who knows? If parents focus only on survival, rather than on mentoring, their offspring may never move beyond trying to survive themselves. Communities advance when they have something to aspire to.

Maybe apartheid's evils – the loss of self-worth, the demoralising effects of racism and injustice, followed by dashed hopes and unfulfilled promises – have done this to us. Some of us cannot conceive of long-term goals, or of preserving anything when the present is hopeless and the future devoid of promise. Young people can only dream of things that they know about. If they know only that wealth comes from crime, that's what their ideal will become. They must be shown that other opportunities exist. Otherwise what will they dream of?

> Show me the heroes that the youth of your country look up to, and I will tell you the future of your country. – *Idowu Koyenikan, author of* Wealth for all Africans

Revering big talkers and fast-living populists is dangerous because they seldom propose concrete solutions. Instead, they say one thing and deliver another, and like to promote the belief that 'clever' is bad. If you want to take the system down, provide a better alternative at least. At heart I'm an engineer. I want to encourage people to fix things, not to raise false hopes. Engineers often make good CEOs because they have a built-in desire to make things work. They understand the unique details of a problem and how they all come together in a big picture. They are trained to consistently produce successful outcomes.

Microsoft's Satya Nadella, who studied electrical engineering, talks of how corporations must persistently seek new energy and ideas, relevance and renewal by reinventing and adapting and improving, as times change. In *Hit Refresh*, he wrote:

> [. . .] a Fourth Industrial Revolution lies ahead, in which machine intelligence will rival that of humans . . . What will the role of humans become? Will inequality resolve or worsen? How can governments help? What is the role of multinational corporations and their leaders?

The writing is on the wall: millions of individuals will be displaced by automation in the next 50 years, but what's important to remember is that humans are in control. No matter how far into the unknown technology takes us, the drivers will always be irrational, emotional and unpredictable humans. We need to understand and shape the Internet of Things so that artificial intelligence works to our advantage: to make medical diagnoses faster and more accurate, so automated cars change traffic flow, and remote sensors detect water leaks or other potential hazards that are out of human sight.

If a CEO has vision and direction and if employees do their jobs as individual contributors, with values in mind, there should be a unified direction with greater scope for good than for evil.

I told *Milestone Magazine* in July 2018 that Africa sits in a space of potential:

> We need to look at the benefits that stem from the fact we are not fully developed . . . Other highly developed countries may be ahead in some respects, but we have a significant advantage in that we don't have legacy technology and infrastructure to overcome. We can leapfrog the old and into the new while other countries are stuck sweating their assets and seeking a return on investment . . .
>
> It is Africans who will ensure that global technologies are relevant to the market. It is Africans who will leverage the technology of the revolution to resolve challenges and create innovative solutions . . . We need to build partnerships between investors and global organisations so that technologies are relevant on a local level. It will be our understanding of the complexities and layers of Africa that will ensure that we can leverage the potential of the Fourth Industrial Revolution . . .
>
> Let us not aim to be leaders, let us aim to be relevant and equal partners.

Early on in my career, I learned from mentors such as Mpho Letlape and Neil Greenfield, who took a bet on a darkie when nobody else would. More than 30 years later, I still have mentors.

Before I made the decision to leave MTN and move to Altron, I spoke to Sifiso Dabengwa, whose wisdom I value. As usual, he helped me to connect with who I am. He guided me to find my own answers. We meet once a quarter and he gives me a fresh perspective, or confirms that I'm on the right track. One of the greatest values of mentors is their ability to see what you may not be able to and to help navigate a course. Meetings with Sifiso leave me motivated and that's what mentorship is about.

I get a lot of requests via social media such as LinkedIn to mentor people. Obviously I can't accept everyone who asks, but if they are already on the corporate ladder and I can sense that they are motivated by a desire to get ahead, I set up a one-on-one meeting to gain a deeper understanding of what they want from the relationship and why they have chosen me. If I feel I can't offer value, I tell them.

Mentoring someone outside your business gives you a more dispassionate perspective, instead of trying to solve an immediate problem, which is what can happen when you mentor someone who works for you. You shouldn't tell your mentee what to do. All he or she needs is advice and guidance.

One of my mentees is Thapelo Masoko, fund head at a company named Edge Growth. He's articulate, able to impart complex ideas in a simple way, is sporty and reads a lot. He's also quirky, which appeals to my sense of humour. He informed me at one of our sessions that he planned to propose to his girlfriend at the top of Burj Khalifa, the world's tallest building, on a visit to Dubai. A few weeks later came the excited message that she'd accepted him. More romantic than me – proposing to Zoleka on the phone.

*

Changing a company sometimes requires changing the environment too. There is no way that Altron House, an old-fashioned building in Parktown, reflects our values. It's quiet and conservative, which does not reflect our fast-paced industry. Our environment should scream ICT and make us look and feel like we are leading change, which we are.

Financial Mail summed it up after interviewing me for a cover story in October 2018.

> Altron, which has morphed into an ICT player, is horribly out of place in its Parktown, Johannesburg headquarters. A visit to the group head office is a little like stepping back in time. The architecture and furnishings – drab, somewhat kitsch and anything but cutting edge – belong to a dull bank from the early 1980s . . . there's no evidence that an innovative technology company calls this its home.

Midway through 2018 we sold Altron House to a property company and made plans to unite in one campus occupying eight buildings. Strategically, we needed to be together in one location, while preserving the individual identities of the various Altron divisions. We will have common spaces like a canteen, pause areas where employees can have private time or host informal meetings, customer briefing centres and innovation hubs.

As CEO, I don't want to be confined to the best office with lunch served to me at my desk. I need to see my colleagues, eat with my colleagues and connect with them in a campus-type setup, so I can put names to faces. Email and mobile devices are great for keeping businesses connected, but they've had a bad side-effect: a sharp drop in face-to-face communication.

So we've made plans to move to Woodmead, to the site where Deloitte currently has a head office. By mid-2021, three thousand Altronians – knowledge workers – will be in one campus for the first time, united by our purpose to deliver innovation that matters. The prospect excites me.

When I took on the Altron challenge, I knew I was made for this. I had found something to fix, adapt and expand. I was in a position to help build a company that could be good for all of us.

In December 2018, as the lights went out again and front pages carried headlines such as, 'Gordhan's call to arms on Eskom spooks bond investors', there was some positive news in the inside pages of *Business Day*, under the headline 'Winds of change at Altron deliver sunny results and forecasts of strong profits':

> Allied Electronics Corporation (Altron) is almost unrecognisable from two years ago. Gone is the byzantine control structure that was dominated by the Venter family . . .
>
> It has transformed from an operation based on infrastructure physical inputs into a player in the ICT sector. Strong profit growth is expected for the foreseeable future, making Altron a potentially attractive share in the software and computer services sector of the JSE.
>
> After the disposals of a long list of operating divisions, the Altron group makeover has changed it from an incoherent electronics conglomerate into something that knits together with common purpose . . .
>
> CEO Mteto Nyati says many operations within the group

have delivered more than 20% ebitda (earnings before interest, tax, depreciation and amortisation) growth and all the struggling businesses from several years ago are now producing in the double digits . . .

Nyati and his team have lofty ambitions, aiming to double ebitda in five years and become number one in the market place . . .

At about R18, the share price is still a long way off its record high of R51,50 in May 2007, but at least the upward trend appears to be intact. The share price troughed at about R4 in November 2015 and has since more than quadrupled in value . . .

With dividends now resuming and a nice balance between hard and soft currency earnings, there appears to be much promise in this new, slick, lean and mean Altron.

At the end of 2018, Altron was one of the top three companies on the JSE whose shares gained the most in an otherwise tough year.

When people transcend their differences and work together to achieve common goals, greatness is possible. I think South Africa is going to be okay.

My family and I spent our 2018 December holidays in Auckland, Taipei and Guangzhou, learning about the world. Anda made the Dean's List. That is what a nation needs: the next generation doing better than the previous one. Perpetual progress.

Dear Anda

I am delighted to inform you that you earned a place on the Dean's List of the Krieger School of Arts and Sciences because of your strong grades during the Fall 2018 Semester.

Being on the Dean's List is an honor at any school. This is of special note at Johns Hopkins because course work here is so challenging. For you to excel in such a demanding environment is a testament to your intelligence, self-discipline and willingness to work very hard.

We want to see all of our students succeed, and this past semester you have clearly achieved a significant goal. You should be very proud and all of us are here at Hopkins honor you for this achievement.

Beverly Wendland

Office of the Dean
The Johns Hopkins University   3400 N Charles Street   Baltimore, MD 21218   410 516 4065   Fax 410 516 4100

247

Afterword

As President Cyril Ramaphosa said in his State of the Nation address in February 2019:

> The world we now inhabit is changing at a pace and in a manner that is unprecedented in human history. Revolutionary advances in technology are reshaping the way people work and live . . . the way people relate to each other, the way societies function and the way they are governed . . . As a young nation . . . we are faced with a stark choice . . . being overtaken by technological change or harnessing it to serve our developmental aspirations. It is a choice between entrenching inequality or creating shared prosperity through innovation. Unless we adapt, unless we understand the nature of the profound change that is reshaping our world, and . . . embrace the opportunities it presents, the promise of our nation's birth will be forever unfulfilled.

In ICT, opportunities abound. While our customers are grappling with the Fourth Industrial Revolution, we have set ourselves up as their trusted advisors for digital transformation. In a world that will be dominated by artificial intelligence, we see a big role for human beings in driving innovation that matters.

Dingulwazi Makwelo, who began his career at Altron serving tea, was offered a role in our tax department by the group manager Annette Brits: he accepted. Six months down the line, noticing a spring in his step, I asked him how things were going there. He said he had moved to the information technology department, doing end-user support – the first line of help when customers encounter problems with products and programs. His passion for service has extended to technology.

From the sidelines I follow with interest the careers of those who have been part of my working life. After almost five years at the helm of Microsoft SA, Zoaib Hoosen stepped down and handed over to Lillian Barnard. This was a big deal for Microsoft and South Africa. Lillian is the first woman of colour to lead Microsoft SA, and her appointment represented a new era for ICT in our country. Cathy Smith, who was HR director at IBM when I was there, became managing director for SAP Africa. Beyond my circle of former colleagues, Dineo Molefe was appointed managing director for T-Systems South Africa in 2018 and Elizabeth Moreno took over as MD for PC and printer giant, HP Inc. These shifts are moving South African society forward in terms of diversity and inclusion.

ICT is at the forefront of the change.

Cast of Experts

Lot Ndlovu – Labour Relations Manager Afrox; President BMF; CEO People's Bank

Neil Greenfield – Quality Assurance Executive Afrox; Executive BOC; Executive Director Linde

Neville Goldin – HR Director Tastic Rice Corporation

Neil Cumming – Group HR Director Nampak; CEO Nampak

Oupa Magashula – HR Director Nampak; National Commissioner SARS; Chairman CZ Electronics

Mpho Letlape – HR Director IBM SA; HR Director Eskom

Lou Gerstner – Chairman, President and CEO IBM (1993–2002)

Mike Kos – Country General Manager IBM SA (1996–1997)

Sal Faso – Country General Manager IBM SA (1997–1998)

Vito Bonafede – Director Strategic Outsourcing IBM SA (1998–2000)

Dennis Hearon – Country General Manager IBM SA (1998–2000)

Mark Harris – Country General Manager IBM SA (2000–2009); Group CEO Kagiso Media (2013–2018)

Andy Williams – Vice President IBM SMB EMEA

Louis Guelette – Vice President IBM SMB CEMA; Vice President IBM SMB Sales EMEA

Marc Lautenbach – Global General Manager IBM SMB; President and CEO Pitney Bowes Inc.

Mike Daniels – Senior Vice President IBM Global Technology Services (2005–2013)

Johann Weihen – IBM General Manager CEMA

Stewart van Graan – IBM SMB Executive; Country General Manager Dell EMC

Massimo Bonciani – IBM Vice President SMB EMEA

Bruce Ross – GM IBM Global Technology Services UKISA

Steve Cowley – General Manager IBM CEEMEA

Giuseppe Giuliani – IBM Vice President Business Partners EMEA

Ginni Rometty – Senior Vice President IBM Global Business Services; Chairman, President and CEO IBM

Astrid Warren – HR Director Microsoft MEA

Jean-Philippe Courtois – President Microsoft Global Sales

Steve Ballmer – Microsoft's 2nd CEO

Satya Nadella – Microsoft's 3rd CEO

Orlando Ayala – Microsoft Chairman Emerging Businesses

Kevin Turner – Microsoft COO; President and CEO Core Scientific

Ali Faramawy – Corporate Vice President Microsoft MEA; CVP Microsoft Emerging Markets

Kethan Parbhoo – Business Manager Microsoft SA; Chief Market and Operations Officer Microsoft SA

Rob Davies – Minister of Trade and Industry

Tshediso Matona – Director-General Department of Trade and Industry

Sipho Zikode – Deputy Director-General Department of Trade and Industry

Nomonde Mesatywa – BEE Director Department of Trade and Industry

Mvuzo Mtyhobile – BEE Director Department of Trade and Industry

Lillian Barnard – Managing Director Microsoft South Africa (2019–)

Zoaib Hoosen – Managing Director Microsoft South Africa (2014–2019)

Kabelo Makwane – Public Sector Director Microsoft SA; Managing Director Microsoft Nigeria

Chris Roberts – Interim Public Sector Director Microsoft South Africa

Benny Serepong – Original Equipment Manufacturers Director Microsoft South Africa

Melanie Botha – Marketing and Operations Director Microsoft South Africa

Paul Norman – Chief Human Resources and Corporate Affairs Officer MTN Group

Alpheus Mangale – Chief Enterprise Business Officer MTN SA; Group CIO Standard Bank

Jose Dos Santos – Cell C CEO

Rob Shuter – MTN President and Group CEO

Dr Bill Venter – Altron founder

Robbie Venter – Altron Chief Executive (2001–2017)

Mike Lemming – Chairman Altron

Johan Klein – Altron HR Director (2015–2017)

Ahmad Farroukh – CEO MTN South Africa

Benjamin Marais – MTN Chief Information Officer

Babak Fouladi – Chief Technology Officer MTN Group

Giovanni Chiarelli – Chief Information and Technology Officer MTN South Africa

Larry Annetts – Chief Consumer Officer MTN South Africa

Maxwell Nonge – Chief Digital Officer MTN South Africa

Nhlanhla Qwabe – Chief Human Resources Officer MTN South Africa

Ideshini Naidoo – Chief Customer Experience Officer MTN South Africa

Sifiso Dabengwa – President and CEO MTN Group (2010–2015)

Phuthuma Nhleko – Chairman MTN Group

Andrew Holden – Operations Executive Bytes Technology Group; Chief Operations Officer Altron

Collin Govender – Group Executive Shared Services Altron

Dolores Mashishi – Group Executive Human Capital Altron

Zipporah Maubane – Group Executive Marketing & Communications Altron

Jan Oelscher – CEO SGB Smit

Mike Brown – CEO Nedbank

Antony Ball – Chairman Value Capital Partners

Sam Sithole – CEO Value Capital Partners

Bonang Mohale – CEO Business Leadership South Africa

Mzwanele Manyi – Black Management Forum

Jabu Mabuza – Chairman Telkom & Eskom

Grant van der Wal – CEO ISPartners; Managing Director Altron
    Karabina

Doug Woolley – Country General Manager Dell-EMC South Africa

Hamilton Ratshefola – Country General Manager IBM South Africa
    (2015–)

Dr Nkosasana Dlamini-Zuma – Former Minister in the Presidency for
    National Planning

President Thabo Mbeki – South African President (1999–2008)

President Jacob Zuma – South African President (2009–2018)

President Cyril Ramaphosa – South African President (2018–)

Acknowledgements

Education has been an important foundation as I developed into a responsible citizen, with a few derailments along the way. Teachers such as Lumka Nongena, Koko Nogemane, Sister Lane, Shena Seipelo Maqubela (Matthews), Nozizwe Majija, Ms Greer, Mr Embling, Prof. Z Katz and Prof. Roberts kept me in check through tough love.

In the vastly different corporate world, my bosses played an important role in encouraging me to be myself while striving to be a team player. This balance was tricky. It was made easier by Dave Bawden, Neil Greenfield, Stephen Viljoen, Clive Jones, Mike Masterson, Grant Forsdick, Mark Harris, Massimo Bonciani, Ali Faramawy, Sifiso Dabengwa and Phuthuma Nhleko.

In the ups and downs of corporate life, friends have provided guidance and support: Andile Mvinyelwa, Mnikelo Stuurman, Wandi Miza, Hale Qangule, Xolela Mangcu, Mpilo Mbambisa, Mpumi Tyikwe, Kay Ngodwana, Lwandle Dyasi, Sithembele Sigabi, Mfanelo Titus, Qaqambile Njokweni, Loyiso Magqaza, Fezile Dunywa, Mcebisi Booi and Dumisani Bomela.

Complex as my family is, I would not trade it for anything. If I were given a choice to reincarnate this life, I would choose the same family. I have plenty of time and love for Mary Nyati, Nodumo Mtshemla (Nyati), Nombeko Mkentane (Nyati), Nombutho Bam (Nyati), Vulisango Nyati, Sazi Nyati, Fundile Nyati, Pelokazi Madlingozi (Nyati) and Langa Nyati.

I enjoyed the partnership with Jessica Pitchford in bringing this book to life. I would also like to thank NB Publishers, Cape Town, including Na'eemah Masoet, Magda Herbst, Abdeah Davis and Olga Wyngaard for their faith in this project. Thank you also to our editor, Gillian Warren-Brown.

And finally I would like to thank my daughter Anda for encouraging me to step out of my comfort zone, and my dear wife Zoleka for her unconditional love and ongoing support.

Mteto nyati, BSc (Eng), has been group chief executive and executive director of Altron since April 2017. He served as the chief executive officer at MTN South Africa from 2014 to March 2017, where he was responsible for returning the business to growth by overhauling employee engagement and transforming customer experience. Prior to that he was group chief enterprise officer of MTN Group Limited. He joined MTN from Microsoft Corporation, where he was the managing director of Microsoft South Africa from 2008. Beginning in June 2005, he had a twelve-year career at IBM, where he was a director of global technology services for South and Central Africa and served in a number of senior executive roles. He led two large business units at IBM: telecommunications, and small and medium business. He has also served as an independent non-executive director at ADvTECH Ltd. and as a non-executive director of Blue Label Telecoms Limited. In 2004, he was named one of the Yale University's World Fellows. He is the joint winner of 2013 IT Personality of the Year. Mteto holds a BSc in Mechanical Engineering from the University of Natal.